THE
UNIVERSITY OF WINNIPEG
PORTAGE & BALMORAL
WINNIPEG 2, MAN. CANADA

HUNTINGTON LIBRARY PUBLICATIONS

Glances at
CALIFORNIA
1847 ❧ 1853

Diaries and Letters of
WILLIAM RICH HUTTON, SURVEYOR

❧

With a Brief Memoir and Notes by
WILLARD O. WATERS

THE HUNTINGTON LIBRARY · SAN MARINO

1942

Anderson & Ritchie : The Ward Ritchie Press
Los Angeles, California, U.S.A.

Contents

Introductory Note

ABOUT three years ago, through the generous aid of the Friends of the Huntington Library, the Library acquired a collection of ninety-five pencil drawings and water-color sketches, depicting scenes in California in the early years of American occupation and statehood. These drawings were made by William R. Hutton, of Washington D.C., who came to California in 1847 as clerk to his uncle, an army paymaster, and remained nearly six years, employed, after his army engagement, and even before its termination, in surveying, drafting, and clerical work. A selection of the drawings has been published by the Library, under the title, *California, 1847-1852*.

The drawings were purchased from the artist's daughters, Misses Mary A. and Rose Hutton, who still reside at the family home in Montgomery County, Maryland. Correspondence with Miss Mary Hutton, undertaken to learn something about her father's career and the circumstances under which the drawings were made, revealed that a small collection of his letters and diaries, written in California, had been preserved. Opportunity was offered by Miss Hutton for an examination of all of her father's papers, but this was found to be impracticable. Instead, it was necessary to depend upon her selection. She has loaned to the Library, with generous permission for publication, forty letters, six short diaries, and some other, miscellaneous papers. Presumably these are the only papers relating to California that have survived in the family archives, although other letters from California are referred to in those examined. From the material submitted twenty-eight of the letters and four of the diaries have been chosen for publication. They are distributed, by years, as follows:

1847, three diaries	1851, four letters
1848, one letter	1852, six letters
1849, one diary and seven letters	1853, two letters
1850, eight letters	

INTRODUCTORY NOTE

The letters are addressed to members of Hutton's immediate family, or to his uncle, and were, of course, written with no thought of publication. They are perhaps of little importance as contributions to California history, but are interesting for their gossip and their side lights on prominent persons and current events, as well as for their glimpses of life on the ranchos and conditions of overland travel up and down the state. And doubtless there may be gleaned from them some bits of information not previously known, or long since forgotten.

It is regrettable that the first two years of Hutton's stay in California are so meagerly represented in the collection. The drawings, nearly all of which are dated, supplement the letters and diaries, by supplying additional facts concerning his movements.

In transcribing the manuscripts, their spelling has been preserved, but the punctuation and capitalization have been modernized and all superior letters have been lowered.

Bibliographical references in the footnotes are to authors and brief titles, with the exception of Hubert Howe Bancroft's *History of California* (San Francisco, 1884-90), which is cited only by author.

Memoir

WILLIAM RICH HUTTON, the eldest son of James and Salome (Rich) Hutton, was born in Washington, D.C., on March 21, 1826.[1] The father was a clerk in the United States Navy Department. There were four younger children, James Dempsey, Ellen Salome, Nathaniel Henry, and Annie Edwards. William obtained his education in private schools, notably Western Academy, conducted in Washington, 1837-40, by George J. Abbot, and the more famous school of Benjamin Hallowell, at Alexandria, where Robert E. Lee prepared for West Point. Under Hallowell young Hutton apparently received special training in mathematics, drawing, and surveying.

On James Hutton's death, in 1843, his wife's brother, William Rich, came to live with the family. This uncle had spent several years in Spain with an older brother, the well-known bibliographer Obadiah Rich. William Rich was a botanist of some reputation, one of the founders of the Botanic Club of Washington, in 1825, and a joint editor of the *American Botanical Register*, 1825-30. He served as botanist of the United States Exploring Expedition of 1838-42, commanded by Charles Wilkes, and accompanied Lieutenant Emmons' overland expedition from the Columbia River to Upper California, in 1841.[2]

In November, 1846, William Rich was appointed paymaster, with the rank of major, to the United States volunteer troops being sent for the occupation of California. For his nephew William he obtained the position of paymaster's clerk. They left Washington for California in January, 1847, accompanied by William's next younger brother, James, their route being through Richmond, Wilmington, Charleston and Mobile to Panama. Having missed the storeship "Erie," which had sailed

[1] *New England Historical and Genealogical Register*, LXXXIV, 37-38; American Society of Civil Engineers *Transactions*, June, 1908, p. 581.

[2] Max Meisel, *A Bibliography of American Natural History* (New York, 1924-29), Vols. II-III, *passim*.

from Panama, carrying Colonel Richard B. Mason, later military governor of California, they embarked on a British steamer for Callao, Peru, where they were picked up by the sloop of war "Preble," arriving at San Francisco on April 19, and at Monterey four days later. A diary and two letters by William R. Hutton, the latter written on the "Preble" at sea, and a letter from Panama, by James D. Hutton, give an account of the journey, but are omitted here.

Major Rich and his clerk appear to have remained in Monterey until late in June, 1847, when they sailed on the "Lexington" for San Pedro, to pay the volunteers at Los Angeles. At Santa Barbara the "Lexington" stopped and took on board two companies of volunteers that had been ordered to occupy Lower California and Mazatlán. While at Santa Barbara, Hutton made a drawing of the town from the anchorage. Rich and Hutton were landed at San Pedro on July 7, and remained in Los Angeles three weeks. They then returned overland to Santa Barbara, and sailed from there to Monterey, the visit to Los Angeles and return to Monterey being recorded by Hutton in a very much condensed diary. The drawings made during this trip to southern California include two of Santa Barbara, one of San Pedro, and three of Los Angeles.

In September, 1847, Governor Mason, accompanied by his adjutant general Lieutenant William T. Sherman, Major Rich, and Hutton, set out from Monterey on an overland ride to San Francisco. Hutton's brief journal gives some incidents of the journey, which is mentioned in the official correspondence of Mason and Sherman,[3] but not in Sherman's *Memoirs*. After a few days in San Francisco, Rich and Hutton continued on to Sonoma to pay Company C of Stevenson's New York regiment of volunteers, and returned to Monterey by water. Record-

[3]Zachary Taylor, *California and New Mexico. Message from the President* (Washington, 1850), *passim.*

ing his impressions more vividly by sketching than by writing, Hutton made seven drawings while on this trip—two of San Juan Bautista Mission, four of San Francisco and the Bay, and one of redwood trees near Rancho Corte-Madera, in what is now Marin County.

Early in July, 1847, two companies (A and B) of the New York regiment, under command of Lieutenant Colonel Henry S. Burton, had sailed from Santa Barbara for La Paz, Lower California. In October, Major Rich and Hutton were ordered south to pay these troops. On the way down the coast stops were made at Los Angeles and San Diego to pay the volunteers stationed there. One of Hutton's disappointingly brief journals is his only record of the voyage from Monterey to Cape San Lucas, October 22-November 12, 1847. But among his drawings (omitted from the published volume) are a dozen made during the three months' stay with Burton's command at La Paz and with the American squadron at Mazatlán. These include five of Mazatlán, five of La Paz, and two of Mexican birds. The dated drawings indicate that Hutton was at Mazatlán in November, 1847, at La Paz in January, 1848, and again at Mazatlán in February. There was also found among his papers a four-page manuscript, in his own hand, with the heading, "Battle of La Paz—From the Journal of an Officer." This is an account, authorship unknown, of events at La Paz, November 16-30, 1847, and is followed by extracts from the report of Lieutenant Charles Heywood on the defense of San José del Cabo, and miscellaneous notes, perhaps by Hutton, of operations at Guaymas and La Paz. The Huntington Library has a photostatic copy of the manuscript.

In January, 1848, Lieutenant Colonel Burton reported from La Paz to Adjutant General Sherman, at Monterey, that he was sending a captured Mexican flag by Major Rich,[4] but Hutton,

[4]James K. Polk, *Message, . . . December 5, 1848* (Washington, 1848), p. 112.

and probably Rich, did not leave Mazatlán before February. On March 15 they were in San Diego, paying off the re-enlisted Mormon volunteers, who had just been discharged.[5] Major Rich arrived in Monterey two weeks later, as stated by Governor Mason in a report to the adjutant general in Washington: "Such is the difficulty of communication, Major Rich left this port on the 22d of October last to make a payment at La Paz, and did not return until the 29th of March. He was fortunate in getting back so soon, as the general probability was that he would have to return via the Sandwich Islands."[6] For some reason Hutton did not accompany his uncle to Monterey, but remained in southern California until May, according to his letter of May 19, 1848. While in the south he made five drawings, during March and April—two of Los Angeles and three of San Luis Rey Mission.

At the end of June, 1848, Rich and Hutton journeyed again to Los Angeles on pay duty. Information is lacking as to their movements between June 30 and August 8, but Hutton's accounts indicate that Los Angeles was the most southerly post visited. On August 8 he spent the day at San Gabriel Mission, in company with Lieutenant John McHenry Hollingsworth, of Company G of the New York regiment, and made drawings, three of which he gave to Hollingsworth. The latter's journal, published in 1923, mentions the visit and the "sketches," and also records that Major Rich left Los Angeles the next day for San Pedro, to embark for Monterey.[7] On August 6 Governor Mason had received official news of the ratification of the treaty

[5]Daniel Tyler, *A Concise History of the Mormon Battalion* ([n.p.] 1881), p. 331.

[6]Taylor, *op. cit.*, p. 465.

[7]California Historical Society *Quarterly*, I, 255. Through the courtesy of that society the Huntington Library has received photostatic copies of these drawings, one showing the main building of the mission, and two others (on one sheet) depicting adobe buildings, presumably connected with the mission, but without title.

of peace with Mexico, and at once issued orders for the payment and discharge of all the volunteer soldiers in California. Major Rich and Hutton proceeded directly from San Pedro to San Francisco, where they arrived on August 21, and made a payment, returning to Monterey a week later. They were immediately ordered south, again, to pay the soldiers awaiting discharge at Santa Barbara, Los Angeles, and San Diego. Two drawings of Santa Barbara Mission, in the Hutton collection, are dated 1848 and were probably made at the end of August or early in September. Uncle and nephew returned to Monterey on October 18. So far as appears from Hutton's accounts they were not on traveling duty again until March, 1849. There are eight Hutton drawings, quite certainly made during this period, showing scenes in and around Monterey. Two of them are dated in November, 1848.

Nothing has been found concerning the activities of the two men from November, 1848, until the spring of 1849, when Hutton made an official journey through the gold region. Evidence is lacking as to whether Major Rich accompanied him. Hutton's claim for subsistence while on the journey covers the period, March 17-May 22, and states that the route was "from Monterey to Sutter's & Far West (Ft. Kearney), and returning, 67 [days]." A military post named Camp Far West was established in 1849 on Bear Creek, ten miles above its junction with Feather River. Major General Persifor F. Smith (commanding the Pacific Division), in a report dated October 7, 1849, stated that a detachment of troops under Major J. J. B. Kingsbury had been ordered to this post, but by September 1 had proceeded no farther than Sutter's Fort. The post was finally established in September and occupied by a detachment of the second infantry, commanded by Captain Hannibal Day.[8] Why an

[8]George W. Crawford, *Report of the Secretary of War, Communicating Information in Relation to the Geology and Topography of California* (Wash-

officer of the Pay Department was sent to a frontier post, evidently planned but not yet occupied by its garrison, has not been ascertained, but Hutton's claim for subsistence, certified by William Rich, and filed with the Treasury Department in 1851, seems to indicate that the trip was actually made. Since the diary published below covers only 24 of the 67 days reported, the probability is that the first and last parts have been lost. The part preserved records a journey from San Francisco to Sutter's Fort, Mormon Island, Sutter's Mill (Coloma), and thence south to Angel's Camp and Stanislaus. The other persons composing the party are not named. The brief entries show that the writer was more interested in the physical aspects of the country, and its fauna and flora, than in the doings of the gold seekers. Drawings of Sutter's Fort, Mormon Island, Sutter's Saw Mill, Dry Creek, and Angel's Camp, all dated, form an additional record of the journey.

By the spring of 1849 the influx of gold seekers into California had brought about so sharp a rise in prices that the army officers and others in government service found their salaries quite inadequate to meet living costs. Recognizing the situation, General Smith encouraged some of the younger officers, among them Lieutenants William T. Sherman and Edward O. C. Ord, to accept private employment, such as land surveying. Sherman and Ord surveyed a ranch, on the Cosumnes River, owned by William E. P. Hartnell of Monterey, and were also engaged to survey several town sites.[9] In May, 1849, the military gov-

ington, 1850), p. 81; Thomas S. Jesup, *Annual Report of the Quartermaster General, . . . 1849-50* (Washington, 1851), pp. 136-37.

[9]Sherman, in his *Memoirs* (4th ed.; New York, 1892), I, 101-4, says that a "young citizen named Seton" was employed on the survey of the ranch. Ord and Sherman received land for their services, but Seton was paid in cash. Is it possible that this assistant was really William R. Hutton, Sherman's recollection of the name, after the lapse of years, having been at fault? Certainly, Hutton was somewhat closely associated with Ord, Halleck, and Sherman during the years 1847-49.

ernor, Major General Bennet Riley, wrote to the alcalde of Los Angeles with regard to the sale of the pueblo lands, advising that a survey be made and a map prepared.[10] On June 9 the *ayuntamiento* adopted a resolution requesting the governor to send a surveyor to do the work. As a result Lieutenant Ord was recommended, and he selected William R. Hutton as his assistant. Seven letters written by Hutton to his uncle in Monterey furnish interesting details of the experiences of the two surveyors in the southern pueblo during the summer of 1849. Some of young Hutton's exceedingly frank comments on Los Angeles officials may perhaps reflect a not uncommon attitude of the newly arrived, energetic Americans toward the easy-going *paisanos*.

Although, with the war's ending in 1848, the volunteer troops had been disbanded, Major Rich was continued in the service, as paymaster, until October 31, 1849, when he was honorably discharged. Hutton's appointment had been terminated two months earlier. Rich left for Washington, probably in September. Hutton, after completing his work with Ord in Los Angeles, returned to Monterey and seems to have found other governmental employment for a time. He wrote in November, in one of his letters, not printed here: "My present intention is to remain in the adjutant's office until spring, & then go surveying wherever I can find work, probably south." His letters indicate that he was in Monterey until May, 1850, when he set out on a journey to San Luis Obispo, described in the letter of May 24. Whatever were the "expectations" referred to in that letter, the journey actually led to an engagement to survey the 38,000-acre ranch of William G. Dana, and probably, through the influence of Dana and his future son-in-law, Henry A. Tefft, to other surveying, public and private. Notwithstanding the disclaimer in his letter, Hutton did accept

[10]Taylor, *op. cit.*, pp. 764-65, 767; Los Angeles archives.

an appointment as county surveyor of San Luis Obispo County, made by the court of sessions at its first meeting, in July, 1850. At its second meeting, in August, the court granted Hutton's petition for a license to survey and make a map of the town of San Luis Obispo. The survey was actually made, but the original map, the first of San Luis Obispo, has disappeared.[11] Hutton's appointment as county surveyor was confirmed at the regular election of September, 1850. During the latter part of that year he surveyed three ranches in the county, for Captain John Wilson, an early settler and large landowner. Hutton's drawings made in 1850 include two of San Luis Obispo Mission, one of the town of San Luis Obispo, two of Wilson's Rancho Cañada de los Osos, and one of a surveying camp, whose location is not indicated.

Hutton continued to serve as county surveyor until August 4, 1851, when he resigned. In May and June, 1851, he was also engaged in surveying, for Francis Z. Branch (one of the largest landowners in San Luis Obispo County), two of his ranches, Santa Manuela and Huer-Huero. It was while he was at Santa Manuela that Hutton took part in the exciting chase after Indian horse-thieves, described in his letter of May 18. Among his drawings are two views of Rancho Santa Manuela, and one entitled, "Huehuero–June 4/51–my camp in the mountains."

In September, 1851, he was back in Monterey, as shown by a dated drawing of the view from Monterey Redoubt. By October he was established at the New Almaden Quicksilver Mine, in Santa Clara County, as assistant to his friend Captain Henry W. Halleck, who had become director-general of the mine in 1850. During the remainder of his stay in California Hutton was employed as clerk, draftsman, and surveyor, dividing his time between the mine and San Francisco, where Halleck was

[11] *History of San Luis Obispo County* (Oakland, 1883), pp. 131, 133, 356; letter to the present editor from M. A. Fitzgerald, San Luis Obispo, July 31, 1940.

a member of the law firm of Halleck, Peachy, Billings & Park. In August, 1852, Halleck and Hutton went to Los Angeles to attend a meeting of the United States Commission for ascertaining and settling private land claims in California,[12] and while in the south visited the Mormon settlement of San Bernardino, early in October. They returned to San Francisco in December, stopping at Santa Barbara on the way. In 1851 Hutton made two drawings of New Almaden and two of San Francisco Bay; in 1852, five of New Almaden, four of Los Angeles, three of San Bernardino, and two of Santa Barbara and the Mission. None of his California drawings in the Huntington Library is dated after 1852.

Having decided to leave California, Hutton carried out the plan, mentioned in his letter of February 15, 1853, to return East by way of Mexico. On March 16 he sailed from San Francisco on the "Golden Gate," arriving at Acapulco a week later. From Acapulco he traveled overland to the city of Mexico, where his uncle, William Rich, had been secretary of the American Legation since January, 1852. Hutton kept a diary of the journey and of his stay in the capital, where he remained several weeks and attended the inauguration of General Santa Anna as president, on April 20.

Home again in Washington, the young surveyor entered upon the profession of civil engineering, which he was to follow with distinction for nearly fifty years. His first engagement was that of assistant engineer on the survey of the projected Metropolitan Railroad, chartered in 1853, to connect Washington with the main line of the Baltimore and Ohio Railroad.

In 1852 and 1853 Congress had made appropriations for a

[12] *Los Angeles Star*, Aug. 28, 1852.

water supply for the city of Washington, and Captain Montgomery C. Meigs, of the engineer corps of the army, had been placed in charge. In May, 1855, Hutton applied for and received a letter of recommendation from his friend and former employer, Henry W. Halleck,[13] which led to his appointment as assistant engineer on the Washington Aqueduct. In this position, and later as division engineer, he worked under Captain Meigs until the spring of 1861, when, with the breaking out of the Civil War, the latter was appointed quartermaster general and work on the aqueduct was suspended. In July, 1862, Congress transferred supervision of the aqueduct from the War Department to the Department of the Interior, and Hutton was appointed chief engineer. It was just after his appointment that there occurred the incident of the removal from Cabin John Bridge, which carries the aqueduct over a deep ravine, of the name of Jefferson Davis, Secretary of War in 1853. For that act Hutton was not responsible, since the name was removed by the contractor at the direct request of Caleb B. Smith, Secretary of the Interior.[14] It was restored to the bridge in 1909, by direction of President Theodore Roosevelt.

During the Civil War, despite the position he held, Mr. Hutton's sympathies were with the South, and he did not conceal his views. Although at one time threatened with arrest, the frank avowal of his feelings, and perhaps the friendship of General Halleck, protected him.[15]

By the close of the war his reputation as an engineer of ability was established. For the purpose of the present memoir it will suffice merely to list the principal engineering works

[13]Photostatic copy in Huntington Library.

[14]William T. S. Curtis, "Cabin John Bridge," in Columbia Historical Society *Records,* II, 293-307.

[15]Letter from Miss Mary A. Hutton, Nov. 24, 1939.

with which he was connected during the next thirty-five years. They were as follows:

Chief engineer of the Annapolis Water Works, 1865-66

Chief engineer of the Chesapeake and Ohio Canal, 1869-71, and its consulting engineer, 1871-80

Chief engineer of the Western Maryland Railroad, 1871-74

Designer and superintendent of the government locks and movable dams on the Great Kanawha River, West Virginia, 1874-78 (received a diploma of honor from the Paris Exposition of 1878 for the designs)

Consulting engineer on the Croton Aqueduct, New York City, 1886

Consulting engineer of the Colorado Midland Railway, 1886-89

Designer and chief engineer of the Washington Bridge over the Harlem River, New York City, 1886-89

Member of the United States board on removal of obstructions at the Dalles of the Columbia River, 1888-89

Chief engineer of the Hudson River Tunnel, 1889-91

In 1900 he was one of four prominent engineers invited to submit designs for the proposed memorial bridge, across the Potomac River, from Washington to Arlington, Virginia. Two different designs were submitted by him, and one of them was awarded second place.

Mr. Hutton was for many years a member and officer of the American Society of Civil Engineers, and held membership in the engineering societies of Great Britain and France.

In 1855 he married Miss Mary Augusta Clopper, of an old Maryland family. To them were born five children, of whom three daughters, Mary A., Rose, and Mrs. Caulfield, are still living, the two former at the family residence in Montgomery County, Maryland. It was there that Mr. Hutton died on December 11, 1901.

He was a member of the Century Association of New York City from 1880 until his death. In the Report of the Association for 1901 the following tribute is paid to his memory:

> [He] became a familiar and always welcome frequenter of the Century. He presented a combination of qualities peculiar perhaps to the southern part of our country, and not very frequent even there, of capacity for sustained and independent intellectual labor, with an earnest zest for the occupations of refined leisure, a taste for many varieties of literature,—foreign as well as English,—and an unfailing gentleness and sympathy and modesty of manner. . . .
>
> His earliest experience was on the Pacific coast in the days of military exploration, and his conversation in later years was often enriched with the most interesting and occasionally exciting memories of life among the Spanish-Americans and the Indians. . . .

GLANCES AT CALIFORNIA

Diaries and Letters

Diaries, 1847

July 7–August 11

July 7', 1847. Left San Pedro & U.S. Ship Lexington on horseback at 9 A.M., escorted by 10 dragoons & a corporal for the safety of the funds. Reached Ciudad de los Angeles at 5 P.M. Saw a large grey wolf near the sheep farms.

27th. Rode out to the Mission of San Gabriel, about 8 miles distant. Had a very pleasant ride but saw only the outside of the building. Uncle went to visit the "tar springs" (rather asphaltum)[16] in the afternoon, with Lt. Stoneman.[17]

29th. Left Los Angeles about 9 A.M. Stopped at Cowenga (8 miles)[18] about 10½ A.M. Mounted again at 12 M. & reached El Rancho del Triunfo[19] after sunset. Managed to get a supper of tea, tortillas, & a beef stew, & then, when we had fixed our bed out doors on an oxhide, went to sleep. (58 m.)

30th. Mounted at sunrise (without breakfast) on fresh horses; mine ran away with me as soon as I was on him but I soon brought him up. After crossing a very high & steep hill we reached Ellwell's ranch,[20] on Santa Clara River, at 9½ A.M. Here we got breakfast & stopped until 2 P.M., then started, crossed Santa Clara River, passed San Buenaventura in an hour,

16La Brea asphalt pits, now in Hancock Park, Los Angeles, and, in recent years, famous for the skeletons of prehistoric animals taken from them.

17George Stoneman (1822-94), cavalry commander in the Civil War, and governor of California, 1883-87.

18Rancho Cahuenga, in the San Fernando Valley, at the north end of Cahuenga Pass. Before secularization of the missions it belonged to San Fernando Mission, but was granted in 1846 to Luis Arenas. (Bancroft, V, 627.)

19In what is now Ventura County, just over the Los Angeles County line. It was formerly owned by the San Fernando Mission. The name originated with Father Juan Crespi during the Portolá expedition, in Jan., 1770. (Herbert E. Bolton, *Fray Juan Crespi* [Berkeley, 1927], pp. 267-69.)

20Presumably the Rancho Santa Clara del Norte, granted in 1837 to Juan Sánchez. His son-in-law, Robert J. Elwell, may have been living on the ranch in 1847. (William Heath Davis, *Seventy-five Years in California* [San Francisco, 1929], p. 123.)

& were overtaken by night 10 miles from Santa Barbara. We then had to walk our horses, & the road was very hilly, but we reached Santa Barbara at 9½ P.M., & remained there (62 m.) until the

3d August, when we left in the Dale[21] & arrived at Monterey 11' August.

September 20–October 12

20' Sept. Left Monterey, with Gov. Mason & Lt. Sherman, & nooned on Salinas plain. At the river the old mare ran away, with $6,000 in the pack, & gave us a hard hunt 'till we found her among the cattle. Reached St. John's[22] at dark.

21st. Started at 9 A.M., passed a range of hills, the Castro farm,[23] & then, over a perfectly level & thinly wooded country with very little water, to Fisher's ranch.[24] We got supper at the house but slept out under a sycamore to escape fleas.

21' [i.e., 22d]. Left early, passed through Pueblo de S. José, & reached Santa Clara, 3 miles further, by 12 M. Dined with officers of Co. I,[25] then encamped there, & left at four o'clock to go 14 miles farther, where we encamped, bought some meat for supper, & saved our coffee for breakfast on the

22d [23d]. Reached Sanchez[26] by 12 M. & dined there. 6 miles

[21]The U.S. sloop of war "Dale."

[22]San Juan Bautista Mission, of which Hutton made two drawings. A pencil inscription on one of them reads: "Stayed one night here with Sherman & Col. Mason; former couldn't eat guisado [a kind of stew]; had some bits of beef en brochette; after trying bed slept in stack of pea straw. Col. M. eat very little & didn't sleep–fleas. Uncle & I eat & slept."

[23]Rancho San Francisco de las Llagas, granted to Carlos Castro in 1834.

[24]Rancho Laguna Seca, owned by Capt. William Fisher. The visit of Mason's party on this occasion is mentioned in Chester S. Lyman's journal (*Around the Horn to the Sandwich Islands and California, 1845-1850* [New Haven, 1924], pp. 239-40).

[25]Of the 1st regiment of New York volunteers. William E. Shannon was captain of Company I.

[26]Rancho Buri Buri, belonging to the Sánchez family.

farther on, Uncle's horse gave out. We left him & took one of the Colonel's. We reached the Mission[27] at 6 P.M. The Govr. & Lt. S. went in to San F. the same evening.[28]

23d [24th]. Went to San Francisco before breakfast; stopped at Brown's Hotel.[29]

Sept. 28'. Left San F., in a launch, for Sonoma; spent the night on the water.

29th. Reached Sonoma (or, rather, Embarcadero) at noon & walked (3 miles) up to Sonoma.

30th. Left El Embarcadero at 3 P.M. Spent the night on the bay. Reached Corta Madera[30] at 11 A.M. on the

1st October, & left at 1½ P.M.; passed the night, until 2 o'clock, at anchor within ½ mile of San Francisco.

8th. Left in the "Malek Adhel"[31] & went over to Sausalito.

9th. " Sausalito at 12 M., & on the

12th reached Monterey in the afternoon.

October 22–November 12

Oct. 22d, 1847. Left Monterey, in the Southampton,[32] for Santa Barbara, S. Pedro, S. Diego, & S. José.

Oct. 26th. Anchored at Santa Barbara at 2 P.M. Sailed at 9 P.M.

Oct. 28th. Anchored at San Pedro at 4 P.M.

Oct. 29th. Went up to Los Angeles with blank accounts. Saw geese very abundant.

[27]Mission San Francisco de Asís.

[28]The *California Star* of Saturday, Sept. 25, announces the arrival "on Thursday last," of Mason, Rich, and Sherman.

[29]This, the first hotel in San Francisco, was later known as the City Hotel.

[30]Rancho Corte Madera del Presidio, on Tiburon Peninsula, in the present Marin County.

[31]A Mexican armed brig, captured at Mazatlán in Sept., 1846.

[32]U.S. storeship.

Oct. 30th. Uncle came up with an escort of dragoons & $10,000.

October 31st. Paid two companies.[33]

Nov. 1st. Paid the rest & mounted at 3½ P.M. to return; rode down in a heavy rain, reached S. Pedro about 7 P.M. Went on board & sailed at 9 P.M.

Nov. 4th. Arrived at S. Diego at 10 A.M. Walked up to town (Uncle rode). Paid off & came down at 7 P.M. on horseback.[34]

Nov. 5th. Sailed at 12 M. from S. Diego.

Nov. 10. 20 miles south of Isla Margarita. A butterfly came on board at noon—a Colias?—very pale yellow & very little black.

Nov. 12. Saw upright cacti after passing Cape San Lucas, & a thalassidroma,[35] mentioned in my note book, crossing equator (No. 3). Petrels & gulls very abundant.

Letter, 1848

Monterey, Cal., May 19th, 1848. Friday.

My dear Mother,

A mail leaves here tomorrow, or next day, for U.S., via Santa Fé,[36] and as I can't go with it I send this as a substitute. Major Hill[37] arrived yesterday in the Matilda[38] & we have received our letters, tho' I have not yet fairly read them—some not looked at.

[33]Companies E and G of the New York volunteer regiment were stationed at Los Angeles at this time.

[34]San Diego was then garrisoned by the company of re-enlisted Mormon volunteers.

[35]A genus of small petrel.

[36]No record has been found of a mail going from Monterey by way of Santa Fé, after the date of this letter, but the *California Star* of June 10 announced that an overland mail would close at San Francisco on June 12. The letter is postmarked, "St. Louis Mo. Oct. 11."

[37]Maj. Henry Hill, army paymaster, who became a member of the constitutional convention of 1849. (Bancroft, III, 785.)

[38]The arrival of the storeship "Matilda" at Monterey, on May 17, is reported in the *California Star* of May 27.

I am very busy now. I arrived up from our La Paz trip just a week ago, & in the course of two weeks more we will go back, I suppose. I found Uncle had gone to San Francisco, whence he returned on Tuesday last. I have been working very hard to get his accounts ready to send off before we leave for Lower Cala., where by some singular streak of fancy he *prefers* going, though, to be sure, he likes the sea. It will be a 3 months' voyage, in all probability. Jim[39] has not had any work since he recd. his appointment. He has been in Santa Barbara, without the money to get away, until I stopped there in the first part of the month. He then came up in the brig, under wages, & is still in

[39]James D. Hutton, who accompanied his uncle and older brother to California, seeking employment. Although only nineteen years of age, he was engaged in July, 1847, to survey and map the pueblo lands of San José. The Huntington Library has a photostatic copy of the original manuscript agreement for this survey, preserved in the archives of San José. On Oct. 20, 1847, Hutton was appointed by Gov. Mason surveyor for the Southern Department of California. Whether from inexperience, or some other cause, Hutton's survey proved to be extremely inaccurate. Complaint was made to the governor, who suspended his appointment in Jan., 1848, and ordered him to appear at San José to answer the charges. No information has been found concerning the final disposition of the case, which is not mentioned by William R. Hutton in any of the letters obtained from his daughter. In Oct., 1847, the San José pueblo lands were resurveyed by Chester S. Lyman, who had arrived in July from the Hawaiian Islands. In his journal (*op. cit.*, pp. 242, 245, 247), Lyman comments caustically on the Hutton survey. Notwithstanding his suspension, Hutton offered his services as a surveyor, in an advertisement (in Spanish) which ran in the *California Star*, Jan. 29-Mar. 25, 1848. In Sept., 1850, he was elected county clerk of San Luis Obispo County, where William R. Hutton was already county surveyor. James D. Hutton resigned as county clerk in Feb., 1852. No information has been obtained concerning his further career in California, but he remained in the state as late as the fall of 1853. He next appears as topographer and assistant artist with the Raynolds expedition of 1859-60, for the exploration of the Yellowstone River. In 1861 he entered the Confederate army as a topographical engineer, served through the war, and at its close went to Mexico, where he died in 1868. The collection of Hutton drawings includes one by James D. Hutton, with the title, "Benecia City from the anchorage, July 4th, 1848." Miss Mary Hutton reports that other drawings made by her uncle in California were destroyed. The Huntington Library has a small collection of drawings made by James D. Hutton while with the Raynolds expedition, and a photostat reproduction of a daguerreotype portrait of him, dating probably from 1847.

her in S. Francisco. He says he was born for the sea & can never succeed at anything else. I was much pleased to get all the things in the box by the "Charles";[40] you seem to know what to send. . . . Annie's bottle of cologne is very useful to put on flea-bites—that is, the big ones; the small ones we are used to. Thomas a Kempis I was very glad to see. I procured at Mazatlan a Spanish copy but it was not like mine. . . . Major Hill spoke of his being followed in two months by a paymaster to relieve Uncle, & then for home. But I fear he was too soon, that it was not real. Uncle has some fine horses, one an excellent jumper, which he dislikes only on that account and which I like for the same reason, tho' I have barely seen either of the horses, yet.

. . . .

You seem to be uneasy about my health. On shore it is excellent, especially when traveling; at sea, want of exercise & the "sea generally" weakens me, but I soon pick up on land & it does me no harm. When I get home I don't want to see salt water again, & I would go home over the mountains if I could.

The barque Anita, chartered by the Govt., is to take a company of volunteers to La Paz, & return immediately, so that this trip will be shorter than our last.[41]

. . . .

Diary and Letters, 1849

Diary, April 1-24

Left San Francisco Ap. 1/49, 11 A.M. Good wind all day. Entered Strs. of Carquines about 5½ P.M. They are from ¾

[40] An American ship which brought naval stores and a private cargo to Monterey, in 1847. (Bancroft, V, 576-77; Taylor, *op. cit.*, p. 619.)

[41] The projected trip was canceled by Gov. Mason because of Lt. Col. Burton's report that the insurrection in Lower California had been put down. (Taylor, pp. 621-23.)

to 1½ miles wide–high, steep hills on both sides; Benicia,[42] half way thro', on a nearly flat point, with low hills & rolling ground behind & along side; plenty of deep water. At night ran aground in Suisun Bay, which is full of low, tule, salt-marsh islands–on the south side, rolling hills; north, hills and mountains. Next day, lay aground until midnight; next (3d) passed Montezuma[43] (one house), opposite the entrance of the two rivers into the bay. No wood; hilly ground. Entered the Sacramento about 10 A.M. Banks (saw elk on the tule marsh) low, fringed with bushes & tule marshes; toward noon trees appeared; about 1 entered mouth of slue; narrowed (40-80 yds.); very rapid current; banks bordered with a strip of trees–sycamore, alder, willow, & some oak behind low [?] [word not deciphered] & lagoon; ducks & geese plenty (& cuckoo?). 4'. Left slue about 3½ P.M. Entered river again; from 150 to 350 yds. wide; banks wooded with sycamore, oak, alder, willow–very bushy–rosa, rhus,[44] ribes;[45] current pretty rapid; Sylvia aestiva.[46] Saw otters, & purple martin plentiful. 5th. No wind until 3 or 4 P.M. Heard Carolina wren. Character of country same; less trees in some places. 6'. No wind; rapid current. Heard warblers & wrens abundantly; fishhawks & nests; cormorants very plenty yesterday–very few today. Afternoon, wind; arrived at night. 7. Left Embarcadero for S.'s Fort. A town rapidly rising at S.'s. Country flat, & some wood.

[42]Founded in 1847 by Robert Semple, and at first called Francisca. For a time it was a rival of San Francisco, and in 1853-54 was the capital of the state. The Huntington Library has a pencil drawing of the town, made in 1848, as noted above.

[43]A town, projected by Lansford W. Hastings, at the head of Suisun Bay. The one adobe house built by the founder was still standing in 1937. (Mildred B. Hoover, *Historic Spots in California: Counties of the Coast Range* [Stanford University, 1937], pp. 610-11.)

[44]Sumac.

[45]Wild currant.

[46]Yellow warbler.

8'. Windy & cold. Icterus Xanthocephalus.[47]

9. Saw oriole (white band on wing), orange below & above, black & blackish on wings & back.

Apr. 13'. Friday. Left Sutters; road over a level, thinly wooded (parklike) country. Lewis woodpeckers abundant—red belly. Flight strong & sustained; sometimes sails & catches flies. Altogether, a bold, handsome bird. Saw elks. Another woodpecker, with black back & ring round neck; light below; white band on wing & crimson occiput [word or letters not deciphered].

14th. At Mormon Diggings[48] all day. The South Fork has high, hilly banks on both sides & is a deep, rapid stream. The diggings are on a half island, low & covered with stones, & the gold is found several feet below the surface; it is all fine, scale gold.

Left Mormon Island on Sunday, Apr. 15', at 8½ A.M. The soil appears different from day before yesterday's route, being composed almost entirely of red clay—the same as we met before reaching the "Island." The ground is much more hilly & much of the same parklike appearance. About 1 o'clock the ground changed [and] a hard "serpentine" made its appearance, in large quantities, along the hill sides. The latter part of the day the hills were very steep & high and the scenery more grand. Many pines were mixed with the oaks, & in some places stood unmixed. They were of two kinds, P. Sinclairii[49] & a tall, straight one with no lateral branches of any size. The Snowy

[47]Yellowheaded blackbird.

[48]An island in the South Fork of the American River, where two Mormons made the second important discovery of gold, in Mar., 1848.

[49]This name, no longer in use, was apparently first given in honor of Andrew Sinclair, Scotch surgeon and naturalist, by Hooker and Arnott, in their *Botany of Captain Beechey's Voyage . . . to the Pacific . . . 1825-28* (London, 1841). According to Thomas Nuttall's addition to Michaux, *North American Sylva* (Philadelphia, 1859), II, 198, the species *Pinus Sinclairii* is found on the California coast, near Monterey. See also Benjamin D. Jackson, *Index Kewensis* (Oxford, 1893-95), III, 392.

Range in sight part of the way. Arrd. at 5 P.M. at the "Saw Mill"[50]—a pretty place; ten to twenty ([corrected to] 20-30) houses & many tents, & appears a thriving place. The river is about 30-40 yds. wide, & rapid. High & bare hills on both sides; the vally narrow & level; full of tall, straight pines, with some oak, yew, & Pinus Sinclairii.

Apr. 17'. Left mill & walked over the high hills, on the way back to Blue Spring.[51] Left B. Spring at 4½ P.M. After two miles over the hills, a most enchanting view broke upon us. To the right (n. & w.) was the valley of the lower Sacramento, the Sonoma Mts. in the distance; on the left & south, the valley of the San Joaquin, apparently perfectly level, the lines of foliage showing the courses of the streams; in the extreme distance, the mountains of the Coast Range; & in front, over the mouths of the two rivers, the blue height of Mt. Diavalo.[52] The valley is not so flat as it appears, but somewhat rolling; the soil red, clayey, mixed with much gravel stone; & we frequently crossed the dry beds of small streams—the bottoms covered with large stones. The vegetation consisted of immense tracts covered with chryseis[53] & cyanotris,[54] euchroma,[55] & some few other plants but also few in number.

Apr. 19'. Left Amn. R., & reached the Cosumnes about 11½ A.M. Lost wagon by rope breaking, in crossing the river.

April 20'. In camp, river Cosumnes. Saw nest & eggs of Stel-

[50]Sutter's Mill, at Coloma.

[51]No other mention of this place has been found.

[52]Mount Diablo, in the present Contra Costa County.

[53]The name has been applied to the California poppy (*Eschscholtzia californica*). (David Douglas, *Journal . . . during his Travels in North America* [London, 1914], p. 327.)

[54]Probably a misspelling of Ceanothus.

[55]One of the varieties of Castilleia (painted cup, or Indian paint brush). For the use of the earlier name, see Thomas Nuttall, *The Genera of North American Plants* (Philadelphia, 1818), II, 54-55.

ler's jay. Nest on a thick vine, about 6 feet from the ground; sticks outside; lined with grass. Eggs, five–rather flattened at the large end; light-blue, specked with dark brown; at large end, spots running into one large blotch of blackish brown. The valley of the river is here about ½ mile wide, 60-70 feet below the country around & 6-10 feet above the river at high water. The river is about 20-30 yds. wide & 20 feet deep. A good many fish but they won't be caught. The river bottom has a good deal of timber & good clear land; oak & willows prevail.

Apr. 22d. Sunday. Left Cosumne & passed over a gravelly, clayey, hilly country to Hicks'[56] ranch, near Dry Creek, a large rivulet about knee deep. At Hicks', stuck 3 hours in a mudhole. Left & went thro' fertile bottoms till afternoon, then over dry, stony hills, & down again to Dry Creek again & camped. Apl. 23d. Left & crossed high hills to Mokelumne; the last hill down was so steep & sideling that the wagon was unloaded. River narrow & rapid, with high, hilly banks, like Am. Fork. Crossed in canoe, & over very steep hills & barren country to Double Tent camp.[57] Apl. 24'. Left, & came over a very hilly mountain road to Stanislaus (Angel's camp), crossing Calaveras & branch 3 times & 2 others once each. Distances estimated: S. Fork to Cosumne, 25; C. to Hicks', 18; H. to Mokelumne (upper crossing), 12; M. to Double Tent, 8; to Calaveras, 8; C. to Angel's camp,[58] 18 m.; A.'s to Stanislaus, 9 miles.

[56]William Hicks, who came to California in 1843, settled in what is now the Ione Valley, Amador County, in 1848. (Jesse D. Mason, *History of Amador County* [Oakland, 1881], p. 182.)

[57]Presumably a mining camp in the present Calaveras County. The name has not been found elsewhere.

[58]A rich mining camp, named for its first prospector, Henry Angel. It later acquired fame as the scene of Samuel L. Clemens' story, *The Celebrated Jumping Frog of Calaveras County.*

GLANCES AT CALIFORNIA

Letters to William Rich, from Los Angeles
July-September, 1849

Los Angeles, Calfa., July 14', 1849.

Dear Uncle,

I wrote from San Pedro but, as the letter must go first to San Diego, you may receive this before that. We left Santa Barbara on the second of July and the next afternoon arrived. Ord & Garnett[59] started off, early the next morning, for town, and returning the evening of the 5th Lt. O—— told me that he had made a proposal to survey the town for $5,000; that they were anxious to have it done but thought the price too high, but he thought he could make an arrangement; that he wanted me to go up with the instruments, &c., while he went on to San Diego, to attend to some business there and return in *five* days by land. I went first to Mr. Prior's;[60] he received me very kindly & I staid 4 or 5 days, but he would not let me pay anything and I did not like to sponge for one or two months, as Ord will be with me when he returns; and I have now a little room at Wilson's,[61] and eat with him & our relation, Martin,[62] who is concerned in business with him. There is no change of consequence since our last visit. Mr. Prior has been very sick but is now better, and attends partially to the vineyard; he will

[59]Maj. Robert Selden Garnett, afterward a brigadier general in the Confederate army. He arrived in California, with official dispatches, in Apr., 1849.

[60]Nathaniel Miguel Pryor, who came to California with James O. Pattie's party in 1828, and lived in or near Los Angeles from 1830 until his death in 1850. (Bancroft, IV, 785.)

[61]Benjamin Davis Wilson (1811-78), merchant, rancher, first mayor of Los Angeles, and state senator. (John W. Caughey, "Don Benito Wilson," *Huntington Library Quarterly,* II, 285-300.)

[62]This may have been Montgomery Martin, a first lieutenant in Frémont's California battalion, and assemblyman from Los Angeles in the first legislature of California, 1849-50. He had business relations with Wilson and Abel Stearns. (Bancroft, IV, 732; Stearns papers in Huntington Library, box 128; Wilson papers in Huntington Library.)

never be *well*—his heart is affected. Tell Mat. Stevenson[63] Doña Paula[64] says he made a bet—that she wouldn't have a baby—of two yards of silk to make caps of—and that she has won. By the way, I expect Isidora[65] has not jilted him so bad as he thinks, though she is carrying on a pretty strong flirtation with T [?] Coutz.[66] Mrs. Stearns said Isi would not marry him (Coutts) because her sweetheart was in Monterey. Wilson & Martin[67] have been doing by far the largest business in Los Angeles. Martin is the same as ever—he makes me right mad sometimes with his nonsense. Old Temple[68] tambien is the same, unless perhaps dirtier. He is the only foreigner who was elected to the town council, & they only took him because they wanted a treasurer & were afraid to trust their own people. The two alcaldes,[69] both Californians, are perfect donkeys, I believe, and as every paisano is a pariente of somebody in authority, and the whites men of some standing, the Indians are the only persons punished. They take very little interest in this proclamation,[70] and a very large number will not vote. Most of the foreigners approve it, & Martin is the only one who has shown his *discernment* by talking against it. The people think here, as

[63]Capt. Matthew R. Stevenson, 1st regiment, New York volunteers. (Bancroft, V, 735.)

[64]Probably Felipe Paula, second wife of Nathaniel Pryor.

[65]Isidora Bandini, sister of Mrs. Abel Stearns, and later the wife of Cave J. Couts.

[66]Lt. Cave J. Couts (1821-74), 1st U.S. dragoons. (Bancroft, II, 770.)

[67]Benjamin D. Wilson and Albert Packard formed a partnership, about 1844, which was dissolved near the end of 1851. The Wilson papers in the Huntington Library include several papers of this firm, dated in 1850 and 1851, but none of the firm of Wilson & Martin.

[68]John (or Jonathan) Temple (1798?-1866), *síndico* of the *ayuntamiento*. (Bancroft, V, 745.)

[69]The alcaldes in office at this time were José del Carmen Lugo and Juan Sepúlveda.

[70]Gov. Riley's proclamation of June 3, 1849, providing for election of delegates to a constitutional convention to be held at Monterey.

in Sta. Barbara, that they are not allowed a sufficient number of delegates, and do not like the uncertainty of choosing supernumeraries. They cannot find enough men for their allowance. Some want to have Frémont, who is daily expected, and let the rest be persons who will vote as he says. The sale of the Chino ranch by Williams to Frémont cannot hold, as the property belongs to Williams's children by his first wife, old Lugo's daughter.[71]

Mr. Ord has now been gone eight days; I cannot think what detains him. He may wait to come up in the vessel which will stop at San Pedro for Capt. Kane[72] & his wife. I hardly think he will get this survey. Last summer, Hall[73] offered to do it for $600, and they cannot think of anything like Ord's price, though they want the four leagues square of town land measured & marked off. We can get plenty of ranches, & such work, near Santa Barbara, I think, and it pays as well. Pray ask Capt. Halleck what are the limits of a pueblo. By tradition they are entitled to four leagues square, but there is no law or title in this part of the country to show the right to a yard of ground, except the law ordering this establishment, which specifies nothing.[74]

[71]Rancho Santa Ana del Chino, granted in 1841 to Antonio María Lugo, who, in the same year, deeded half of it to his son-in-law, Isaac Williams. In 1847, 1849, and 1850 Williams negotiated with the Mormons for the sale of the ranch. Frémont is said to have offered $200,000 for it. (George W. and Helen P. Beattie, *Heritage of the Valley; San Bernardino's First Century* [Pasadena, 1939], pp. 120-37; Jefferson Davis, *Reports of Explorations and Surveys . . . for a Railroad . . . to the Pacific Ocean*, III [Washington, 1856], p. 135.)

[72]Elias Kent Kane (1820?-53), 2d regiment of dragoons; on quartermaster duty, 1848-52. (Bancroft, IV, 696.)

[73]Possibly John Halls, civil engineer and land surveyor, who arrived in California in Jan., 1847, and advertised in the *California Star*, Sept., 1847-June, 1848. (*Ibid.*, III, 774.) Hall is also mentioned in Hutton's letter of Aug. 5, 1849.

[74]Halleck had prepared a "Report on the Laws and Regulations Relative to Grants or Sales of Public Lands in California," dated Mar. 1, 1849, which is printed in Taylor, *op. cit.*, pp. 118-82.

Dr. Foster[75] told me, a day or two since, that there are probably more valuable books & papers in the Mission of San Diego than in any other.

Tell Mrs. Canby[76] & Lt. Murray[77] I turned their messages over to Major Garnett. Has Dr. Griffin[78] resigned? They say, here, he is going to do so and establish himself here with Dr. Hope.[79]

There is no fruit ripe yet in town—a little at the mission.

Temple talks of having Frémont make their survey if he brings instruments; I can't find out how much they are willing to pay. Ord wanted to get a theodolite in San Diego, and some few other things, and said he would be up in five or six days. He may have found difficulty in buying a horse, as they have all been bought up in that neighborhood for this commission,[80] tho' it does not expect to start. (I will keep this open until an opportunity offers to send it.)

A few days ago, as I was looking over books in Wilson['s sto]re, I saw one marked "Frai Gerundio['s]" "Teatro social." He com[mences] his introduction by speaking of all sorts of ghosts and the [ones that?] appeared to him in particular; some of his articles were hea[ded] the same as in Padre Isla's, such as "Casa de Locos" & some others, but on the title page it was marke[d] "El Siglo XIX." Do you know anything of such a

[75]Stephen Clark Foster (1820-98), alcalde of Los Angeles, 1848-49. (Henry D. Barrows, "Stephen C. Foster," in Historical Society of Southern California *Publications,* IV, 179-83.)

[76]Wife of Maj. Edward R. S. Canby.

[77]Lt. Edward Murray (1820?-74).

[78]Dr. John Strother Griffin (1816-98), assistant surgeon with Kearny's expedition to California, 1846. He became a prominent citizen of Los Angeles. (*Illustrated History of Los Angeles County* [Chicago, 1889], pp. 206-7.)

[79]Dr. Alexander W. Hope was a resident of Los Angeles, 1848-56. (Bancroft, III, 787.)

[80]Probably refers to the commission appointed in Jan., 1849, to survey the boundary between the United States and Mexico.

book? It completely fooled me at first. It is in the same style as the real one, but "muy moderna."

I have a chance to send this tonight. Remember me to all my friends, the Col. & Capt. Halleck, the Doña,[81] & Mrs. Canby; & let me know how you come on.

Los Angeles, July 19th, 1849.

My dear Uncle,

I received yours of the 8th, yesterday, with much pleasure. To the Colonel[82] "y su novia muchos y felices años," or the usual compliments; I sincerely wish them all happiness. Has Capt. Halleck rented our house for himself? I am glad you do not go to Sacramento & San Joaquin; if you want to leave Monterey for any place but home I should regret having come away. Ord will probably leave in the end of September for the U.S.; he wants to be in Monterey by the 1st, though I do not believe he can. I think it is certain we will survey this town; at all events, the bargain will be concluded before I send this to the beach this afternoon. He gets $3,000 in money, which was advanced by merchants, as they thought his estimate of town lots too low. We go from the hills to the river & from the grave yard as far as the last house south of town, marking out a good many new squares back of the volunteer barracks;[83] in addition, we are to measure 4 leagues, north, south, east, & west of the church, & mark the corners as those of the town

[81]Doña María de las Augustias, wife of Manuel Jimeno Casarin, of Monterey. (*Ibid.*, IV, 692.)

[82]It is uncertain to whom Hutton refers; possibly to Capt. Henry S. Burton, who held the rank of lieutenant colonel while in command in Lower California. Burton had recently married Señorita María Amparo Ruiz, and Hutton was groomsman at the wedding. (Private information from Miss Mary A. Hutton.)

[83]This building, at the corner of Alameda and Macy Streets, was Wilson's home until 1856, when it was sold to the Sisters of Charity for a school and orphan asylum.

lands. We will then go to Santa Clara River, as soon as possible, & finish Don Manuel's ranch.[84] If I were to keep at this I could not work in the winter, I suppose; that would be a disadvantage. I had all my drawing things stolen from my room a couple of nights since, while at supper, through the window, but expect to recover them. In my idle time I have been looking over books in the stores: Temple has Guzman de Alfarache (Madrid ed.), 1 volume, price $5; Quintana, Vidas de españoles celebres, 2 vols., $4.00; Mendoza, Guerra de Granada, 1 vol., $3.00. If you think it worth while that I should buy any of them, mention it in your next letter. I made one small foolish purchase (though I can turn it to advantage now) and am getting as close as the dickens. I feel as if I wouldn't buy anything if I could help it. I haven't spent much ($5), except for expenses which will be reimbursed. The weather is very hot here, though it has been cold & foggy and the season very backward. There are scarcely any pears ripe and no other fruit. I left Prior's and came up to Wilson's, where I can pay my board, by Mr. Ord's advice; but he went to Prior's, as soon as he came, and will probably stay there. It is by far the most comfortable place, but I think he will have to come up town when he gets to work.

Did Capt. Halleck say anything to you about me or my letter? & where do you live now that the house is rented? If I can find out, before you start, when you will go, I will be up before that time.

Pray, how can I have a room any where if I have to roam so much? I do not suggest this as an objection, but to receive advice. There are other things I was about to write, but, as I must see you before you go, we can talk them over.

There is a constant stream of persons coming in, from all parts of the U.S., via Santa Fé; they think they have suffered

[84]Rancho Santa Paula y Saticoy, in the present Ventura County, granted in 1843 to Manuel Jimeno Casarin, of Monterey.

more than ever human beings did before. Shoto[85] brought in a party. He said he was afraid they would eat him, sometimes; they started with plenty of provision, but wasted it, and, when they found there was a probability of being out of grub, they determined to eat enough while it lasted. Shoto shared everything with them & was horrified that they should eat snakes, horse meat, &c. He says they were never more than 14 hours without food. He found deer where they had never been heard of before. Another party were obliged to live three weeks on *pumpkins* & *beans*, and thought never men suffered as they suffered. Kit Carson & Maxwell[86] are bringing out a very large emigration by the Spanish Trail.[87] Kit & Maxwell want to buy Warner's ranch[88] & settle it. It is said 20,000 persons will leave Independence, this year, for California.

Endart's (?) brig[89] has arrived from Callao & goes to Monterey probably. He has not much of consequence, *I believe.*

An order has been recd. from Gen. Riley for the judges of the tribunal superior to proceed to Monterey, immediately on their election;[90] as they understand it here, they cannot comply

[85]Apparently the reference is to a member of the well-known Chouteau family of Missouri, perhaps the B. Chouteau whose arrival at Santa Fé from California, on Aug. 15, 1848, was reported in the *Santa Fé Republican* of that date. (*Southern Trails to California in 1849*, ed. Ralph P. Bieber [Glendale, Calif., 1937], p. 67.) The name Benito Chouteau appears in the list of voters of Los Angeles at the election of Nov. 13, 1849. (Los Angeles County records [MS], 1840-50, p. 861.)

[86]Lucien Bonaparte Maxwell, friend of Christopher Carson, and owner of the immense Beaubien and Miranda grant, better known as the Maxwell grant, in New Mexico.

[87]No record has been found of such an expedition. Carson, in his *Autobiography* (Chicago, 1935), does not mention visiting California between 1848 and 1853.

[88]The Rancho San José del Valle, in the present San Diego County, granted to Jonathan T. Warner in 1845.

[89]Probably the "Farisco," a Mexican brig, José D. Yndart, master. (Bancroft, IV, 565.)

[90]Refers to Gov. Riley's circular, dated July 2, 1849. (Taylor, p. 795.)

with it, as the votes of each town must be sent to Monterey to be decided.

I hear Lt. Murray & his lady are at San Diego. Mr. Ord wants this now. He says I had better tell you I will be down here some time, as they want San Diego surveyed,[91] &, I believe, Santa Barbara[92] & several ranches in its neighborhood. If you should go before I come up, if I can get down to San Diego I will be on the beach as soon as I hear of the steamer.

Give my respects to the Doña & Mrs. Canby, to Capt. Halleck, the Colonel, & Maj. C.–also remember me to the young ladies.

I am sometimes sorry that I left Monterey so soon, but it does me good, I think, to be alone and look back over what has passed. I *think* much more, now, than I did before I came away.

. . . .

P.S. If you can *encontrar* any pencils, drawing paper, or India ink, & have a chance to send me some, please do so. I left some ink in a tin percussion-cap box, I think.

Los Angeles, July 29th, 1849.

Dear Uncle,

I have written several times to you, but the two last letters have come back, and I will send this to San Diego, so that if you go home soon you may know what has become of me. Mr. Ord, after a good deal of haggling with Johnny Temple, contracted to do the survey of this place for $3,000. We commenced last Monday, & have gone from the church to the last house on the main street, about 1¼ miles; thence west to the hills, laying off in squares the plain; then to the vineyards, for

[91]The town of San Diego was surveyed, in 1849, by Lt. Cave J. Couts. (Harry C. Hopkins, *History of San Diego* [San Diego, 1929], pp. 155, 223.)

[92]The first survey of Santa Barbara, after the American occupation, was made by Capt. Salisbury Haley in 1851.

he is to include all the cultivated ground between the hills & the river, within two miles of the church. We have gone over all south & west of a line from the Plaza to Bell's,[93] then to Prior's, & from the east through a lane to the river. We work much faster than I expected. We will be through the field work in a week or ten days more, but there is a good two weeks' work in the drawing. He has employed three Americans to assist as chain & signal bearers, &c., from the great number daily arriving. We have only used his compass, which works beautifully, but in some cases I think mine would be better. I will be badly off for a chain, when I leave him, as mine stretches. Before I commenced work I imagined, as usual, that I had the worst kind of sicknesses, but, since then, I never have been better.

The Americans of this place, wishing to have some municipal body here, some time ago procured an election, with much difficulty, but were not strong enough to elect anybody.[94] The alcaldes & ayuntamiento are a mighty poor set. A few days ago one American (the mail rider)[95] bullied the whole set, insulted the alcalde, and scared all the Californians in town. They could not raise constables who would dare to take him.

We have rather pleasant weather, though pretty warm in the forenoon. I find I am not more fatigued than Mr. Ord, & not so much as the rest of the party, by the sun and sand.

I don't recollect whether I have *sent* a letter since I received yours of the 8th (?). I am glad that you have no idea of going up the Sacramento & San Joaquin, but I did not think you

[93]Bell's Row, a large, two-story, adobe building at the corner of Los Angeles and Aliso Streets. It was built by Alexander Bell, an early merchant (who arrived in Los Angeles in 1842), and was said to be the finest house in California at the time of its erection.

[94]At an election held in Dec., 1848, Abel Stearns was elected alcalde, serving until May 21, 1849.

[95]In 1849 there was a military express mail, with three riders: one between San Francisco and Monterey, the second between Monterey and William G. Dana's Nipomo Rancho, and the third between Dana's and Los Angeles. (Taylor, pp. 878-79.)

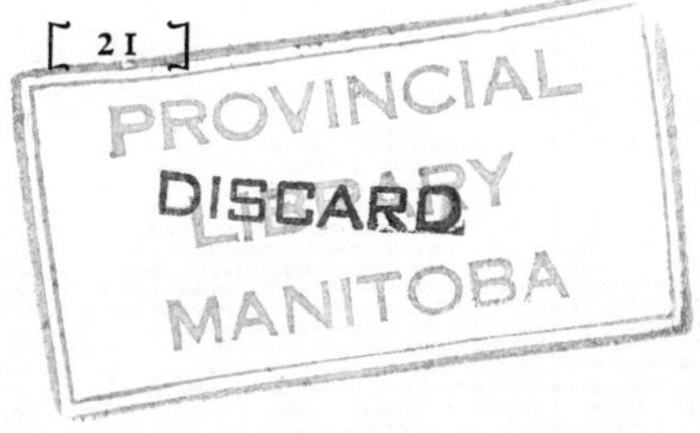

would. I don't know whether I will be able to be in Monterey by the 1st of Septr., unless I hear that you are going, but if I am anywhere near San Diego or Santa Barbara I will be on the beach when the steamer stops, so that I will not lose any chance. If you are going on the 1' August this is too late.

I will have need of a good ruler (steel is best), a chain, drawing paper, pencils, & ink, if you come across any before you go.

Give my respects to all. To the Colonel and his novia I wish "muchos y felices años." I forget that I am writing this to catch you at San Diego as you pass down. Again I will alter my mind & send it up to Monterey, as I am pretty sure that it would not get on board the steamer to you. So remember me especially to Mrs. Canby & Doña Angustias, if you receive this in Monterey, and que le vaya usted bien. Good bye, dear Uncle.

. . . .

Don Juan Fo[r]ster[96] goes up this afternoon & I send this by him. I enclose two which I have sent once & they have returned to me in place of going to you.

Los Angeles, August 5th, 1849.

It is but a few days, dear Uncle, since I sent several letters which I had written before, but they were always hurried, and, as the mail goes north again tomorrow, I send one prepared more at leisure.

I am *very* well, and hard at work all the week. We have finished the field work, with the exception of four lines to the four winds, from the church as a centre—each line two leagues long. We commence this work tomorrow and, that finished, the plan will be the only thing undone. I have not used my

[96]John (known as Don Juan) Forster (1814?-84), an Englishman, came to Los Angeles in 1833. He married a sister of Andrés and Pío Pico, and became a very large landowner. He lived in San Juan Capistrano from 1844 to 1864, and spent the remainder of his life on his Rancho Santa Margarita, in San Diego County. (Bancroft, III, 744.)

compass at all. Mr. Ord's worked beautifully at first, but latterly it has proved less correct. We observed for the variation of the needle, a few nights since, & found it 12° 44′ east, but I don't think it *very* correct. Mr. O. has written to San Diego for some drawing paper for me. He went down partially to get paper and some books, & those things which he did not forget have gone on to Santa Barbara. He thinks I can get plenty of work in this part of the country. I may at Santa Barbara but I think not here. The best ranches have been surveyed by Hall & O'Farrel,[97] & most of the others by Stearns,[98] & others, in the fashion of the country, with a rope carried by two men on horseback;[99] but the people are satisfied with it. I think I could do very well now; I should work slowly with my instrument but, I think, correctly. I see it is an object with many to work quick, and to my notion they are not so careful as they might be. We met a surveyor from Texas, also a volunteer officer & wounded during the war, who wanted to assist Mr. Ord, but he came too late.

We have no news from above or below, except indistinct rumors. It is reported that the Americans and Chilenos have commenced fighting in the mines & that Generals Smith and Riley have gone up with artillery to stop it[100]—tambien that

[97]Jasper O'Farrell (1822-75), an Irish civil engineer and surveyor, was appointed an official surveyor by Gov. Mason in 1847, and made the first survey of Yerba Buena the same year. (Helen P. Van Sicklen, "Jasper O'Farrell: His Survey of San Francisco," in Society of California Pioneers *Quarterly*, X, 85-97.)

[98]Abel Stearns (1798-1871), a resident of Los Angeles, and perhaps the most prominent citizen of southern California. (Robert G. Cleland, *The Cattle on a Thousand Hills* [San Marino, Calif., 1941], pp. 243-73.)

[99]Dr. Cleland devotes several pages to an account of early methods of running boundary lines in California. (*Ibid.*, pp. 37-41.)

[100]Concerning the ill-feeling existing between American and Chilean miners in California, see: James J. Ayers, *Gold and Sunshine* (Boston, 1922), pp. 46-63; Roberto Hernández Cornejo, *Los Chilenos en San Francisco de California* (Valparaiso, 1930), I, *passim.*

the cholera is raging in San Diego. The first finds more believers than the last. It is also rumored that a rich placer exists near this place. Some gold has been brought in, I believe, & persons on Williams' ranch have more of it. A party has gone out from this place to work it. They have not been heard from since they left.

New crowds are continually arriving from the U.S., by way of Santa Fé, mostly by the Jila route. Many of them are very indignant at Emory[101] that he should have given such a flattering description of the road. He says there is grass where they found none, but I am told by mountain men that a sandhill might form over a grass patch in two weeks. I suspect he must be incorrect in some of his distances, from the information I have received.

The most singular feature in the geography of that part of the country is this new river in the desert this side the Colorado. It comes from the San Berna[r]dino Mountains (probably from a lake said to exist there) and runs *from* the Colorado across the desert and forms a lake, on the other side, which was rapidly increasing and extending towards the foot of the opposite mountains. It is a narrow, deep, and rapid stream, bad for travellers to cross on account of the mud, but a great benefit by shortening the distance to water. It appears to have formerly existed, as there was a slight channel in the same place before.[102]

The steamer arrived at San Pedro yesterday & we have just

[101]Lt. William Hemsley Emory (1811-87), chief engineer of Gen. Kearny's Army of the West, and author of *Notes of a Military Reconnaissance, from Fort Leavenworth, . . . to San Diego* (Washington, 1848).

[102]This stream flows from Volcano Lake, in Lower California, across the international boundary line, and empties its waters into the lower end of the Salton Sea. Its sudden appearance, recorded by Hutton, was due to its having received, in a flood season, an unusual amount of the overflow of the Colorado River. John R. Bartlett, in his *Personal Narrative of Explorations and Incidents . . . Connected with the United States and Mexican Boundary Commission* (New York, 1854), II, 135, says that the appearance of a supposedly new stream was hailed by passing emigrants "as a miracle and direct interposition of Divine Providence."

heard the fighting report contradicted. No letters have come up yet.

The election was held here on the first & Dr. Foster, Manuel Dominguez, Stearns, José Anto. Carrillo, & supernumerary Hugo Read, were elected.[103]

Don Domingo Indart[104] quiso saber adonde está mi tio, i tiene muchas ganas de verle en Monterey.

My best respects to Mrs. Canby & the Doña and to the gentlemen, & I hope you will take care & not let yourself get sick, which I most fear. A Dios, dear Uncle.

Los Angeles, Aug. 8', 1849.

My dear Uncle,

I have just received your letter of the 1st inst., enclosing three from home. The steamer stopped at San Pedro but, as she left no mail, the letters went down to San Diego & came up by land. You say there is a prospect of another wedding soon; I fear it will be a case of "marry in haste and repent at leisure," but, if they will do such things, "good luck to them." What was the reason *our ladies* were not invited to the baile [on the] 4th? It seems a very strange oversight.

I am glad the deeds for those San José lots are in your keeping. If you think at any time that I had better dispose of them,

[103]The election for selecting delegates to the constitutional convention. Manuel Dominguez was owner of the Rancho San Pedro and held various official positions in Los Angeles and Los Angeles County. (Bancroft, II, 783.) José Antonio Carrillo (1794-1862) was one of the leading Californians of the Mexican period and had represented the province in the Mexican Congress. (Bancroft, II, 745-46.) Hugo Reid (1810?-52) was a native of Scotland and settled in Los Angeles in 1834. He wrote a series of valuable articles on the Indians of Los Angeles County. (Susanna B. Dakin, *A Scotch Paisano* [Berkeley, 1939].) The other two delegates were Stephen Clark Foster and Abel Stearns.

[104]This may refer to José D. Yndart, master of the Mexican brig "Farisco," mentioned in Hutton's letter of July 19, 1849, as "Endart."

before you leave, let me know and I will send you any papers that may be necessary.[105]

How can Maj. Leonard[106] refuse to receive that money? I should suppose he would feel obliged to do so, under the circumstances. I see by Mother's last letter that the General's intention in keeping you out here was to retain you in service—though certainly an unpleasant place to keep you. What a bustling time they seem to have had at home. Lt. Raynolds[107] is an army officer, if I recollect rightly, and not your friend. The sealed letter is from Ben. Homans. He is now at Wheeling, in charge of the magnetic telegraph at that place; he speaks a great deal about *the instrument*, but I could not guess what kind of an instrument it was, until I had finished the letter. His father & Southard are in business in Cincinnati, & his Aunt Sarah (Mrs. Nourse) & her husband are going there very shortly.

Mr. Ord has just received from Santa Barbara a lot of letters, &c., containing, *I believe*, a large quantity of family news and private scandal, but nothing, he says, of real news or information. Major Garnett sent down his Davis's Surveying, which is or will be of great use. There is a book which Davidson[108] left here, "Simms on Instruments," which is very useful at times, and I think I can carry it off when I go.

I wrote home by the last mail, sending the letter by way of San Diego.

I am getting on pretty well here. We have finished the town and vineyards and are now at the "two leagues to the four winds." It was pretty hard work measuring one line (to the

[105]Several lots in San José were bought, for himself and his brother, by James D. Hutton, who surveyed the pueblo lands there in 1847.

[106]Maj. Hiram Leonard, paymaster of volunteers.

[107]Lt. William Franklin Raynolds, of the engineer department. In 1859-60 he was in charge of an expedition for the exploration of the Yellowstone River, on which James D. Hutton served as topographer and assistant artist.

[108]Lt. John W. Davidson (1823-81), 1st regiment, U.S. dragoons.

south) in one day, though the ground was level, for the mustard was *very* tall & thick; the second day, going to the east, we could not finish one, as we had not only mustard but very high hills to go over, but we got through this morning, & after dinner made a start on the west course, which we will finish tomorrow. The north line goes over the top of the high hill beyond the cemetery, & Mr. O. thinks it will take three or four days. After that, however, we have no more field work but sketching. I have plotted a sketch map as we worked, but on cartridge paper which was kept folded & consequently could not be *very* correct.

If Lise's[109] vessel comes in, pray try and get some India ink. I think I can get some drawing paper from San Diego, through Lt. Ord. I think I should have no trouble at all in any common surveying, and will probably get some work near Santa Barbara.

Th[r]e[e] or four days ago we had (or rather one of our party had[)] quite an adventure. I was off, measuring, some distance from the compass but, looking back, saw a man on horseback driving three steers, one of which was pretty mad. As he came near, he made right for the compass; Ord ran to a hill & gully near by, the other man dodged behind the instrument, but the bull went round, and as he (the boy) started to run struck him, in the breast, with his forehead & rolled him heels over head. Fortunately he did not repeat the blow & the man was not so much hurt as scared. A few days afterwards we came upon a crowd of cattle, a long ways from town, & we were all somewhat scared, but we succeeded in frightening them worse than we were.

No fruit has ripened this year, as yet, except a few brevas[110] and fewer pears. The vines are loaded but they won't ripen.

[109]Probably refers to Jacob Primer Leese (1809-92), an early merchant and trader in Los Angeles, San Francisco, and Sonoma. At this time he was absent on a voyage to China. (Helen P. Van Sicklen, "The Leese Scrap Book," in Soc. of Calif. Pioneers *Quarterly*, VIII, 9-37.)

[110]The early fruit of a variety of fig tree.

There is a real Monterey fog out-of-doors, now, & the nights, or rather evenings, are generally foggy.

. . . .

When you see Major Hill remember me to him & thank him for taking the trouble to pay the postage on your last letter & forwarding it to this place. The letter was marked 40¢.

. . . .

Los Angeles, August 19', 1849.

My dear Uncle,

Dr. Foster leaves tomorrow, or next day, for Monterey, with his co-delegates, and I send this by him. Since I last wrote, nothing new has happened. We have finished the field work of the survey and Mr. Ord is drawing the plan; I am sketching the topography. We will be through in about ten days or two weeks. The weather has been very hot and, within the last three or four days, we have had a "right smart sprinkling" of rain, and the sky is now overcast. It is spoken of as a very unusual extension of the rains of Lower California. It is said that, in New Mexico, hills which before the war were left unimproved, on account of the difficulty of irrigation, are now covered with fine crops, the rain being sufficient for them. Travellers are still coming in from the U.S., by way of New Mexico; most of them have had a hard time. I hear that the prices of goods in San Francisco is still high—more so, even, than when we were there last spring. I heard, indirectly, that Davidson had been killed in a quarrel.

A day or two since, Martin said to me, "Frémont has left here an instrument of steel, in a case, which looks like a ruler. What is it?" I went to see & found a beautiful steel ruler—the very thing we wanted—but it was too late to use on this map. I found also a telescope, Munich make, apparently a fine instrument; this is one of those procured with the $30,000 appropriated to continue the survey of California.[111] The rest are in the mountains of New Mexico, and the party (paid, I believe, out of the same money) digging in the mines. A party has been fitted out in New Mexico to go up & recover the instruments left by him. He said that it was very easy to explain why he had not found the gold, & gave, as a reason, that he was looking for plants *on* the surface & not for anything *under* it.

Mr. Ord has written to some of the top. officers at San Diego, to send him some drawing paper, & if the[y] do so I shall fall heir to a part of it when he goes north. I don't think I can get much work *here*, now; at Santa Barbara I may, as Gaspar Oreña[112] told me he had a ranch which ought to be surveyed, and "El Sr. Dn. José Noriega,"[113] who has a good many farms, asked Mr. Ord if he worked cheap. Ord told him *he thought* he did. But the word "cheap" is a very indefinite one. Old Temple has been talking as if Ord was trying [to cheat?] the town of Los Angeles; he bored him to death & delayed everything in the first place, then he inserted in the contract several articles which Ord refused to agree to, and he did not notice them until after he had signed it. Ord told him in plain terms that he thought he was to deal with gentlemen, that if it was not so he wanted to break off as soon as he could, & then Johnny shut up; but he would talk to me sometimes about the work.

[111]A reference to Frémont's fourth expedition, Oct., 1848-Jan., 1849, planned to discover a railway route to the Pacific Coast. An amendment providing $30,000 for the expedition passed the Senate but failed in the House of Representatives, and the necessary funds were apparently raised by private subscription.

[112]Gaspar Oreña was a Spanish trader in California from 1843 or earlier. He was a resident of Santa Barbara and married to a daughter of José de la Guerra y Noriega. (Bancroft, IV, 760.)

[113]José de la Guerra y Noriega (1779-1858), a native of Spain, came to California in 1801 and served for many years as an army officer. He was a resident of Santa Barbara, an influential citizen, and a large landholder. (*Ibid.*, III, 769-71.)

One day he said to me, pointing to a stone at one corner of a square, "Well, you must come here again; here is only one stone; there must be four." I did not say anything, but pointed to the three others, which were plain enough to be seen, only he was looking the wrong way for them. He did such things several times &, after he found that he was always wrong, he kept on his side of the street.

I wish I could send you some of the fine figs we have now. Pears are not good, even those that are ripe, which are very few. Melons are not yet ripe; grapes are just beginning. Going through a vineyard, yesterday, I found a good many bunches with ripe grapes on them, but no entire clusters fit to eat.

I am a little anxious to hear from you, and the result of your letter to General Smith. I expected to have heard by the mail–but, on reflection, it left but a very short time after the date of your last letter, though that has been received some time. I want to hear when you are likely to start. Have you heard anything of the revenue cutter and Jim Overstreet?[114] Almost everybody in these parts picks up a relation, occasionally, among the new comers.

We have just heard a report that the Sonorenians, in revenge for being turned out of the mines, are coming to this place to kill all the Americans here, & that Urrea[115] will head them.

[114]James T. Overstreet, a young man from Washington, D.C., who is mentioned by Hutton in his letter of Jan. 31, 1850, as then living with him in Monterey. In 1851 Overstreet was stationed at the U.S. army barracks at Rancho Santa Ana del Chino, as assistant army surgeon. In 1852 he was one of the clerks of the U.S. Land Commission. He was shot to death in Los Angeles, in the early morning of Feb. 23, 1853, in the course of an attack on the residence of Abel Stearns during a ball held in celebration of Washington's Birthday. (*Census of the City and County of Los Angeles . . . for the Year 1850* [Los Angeles, 1929], p. 97; *Los Angeles Star*, Feb. 26, 1853.)

[115]Presumably Gen. José Urrea, governor of Sonora during the 1840's.

Los Angeles, Sept. 1', 1849.

My dear Uncle,

I received on the 27' your long letters, by Lt. Hamilton,[116] and take advantage of a little spare time to answer them. The longest I burned as directed, after several readings. As to our friend, his behaviour towards me has been as kind as I could expect. There was a good deal of accident in the affair of Mr. Prior's house, and, although he says a great many things about others which I do not like to hear, he has behaved very well towards me. I have had no money transactions with him yet, except to lend, for Major Garnett took all his supply to Santa Barbara & he had not enough to pay the expenses of the survey.

The very day that I received your letters I was thinking of writing to you to see if there was any other occupation I could take up, and if you or Mr. Halleck advises it I will come to Monterey, when you think best. I may get employment in Santa Barbara for a month or two, possibly, but constant occupation cannot be obtained by a surveyor in these parts. If I do not get work at Santa Barbara I will go on with Ord to Monterey. I am afraid I will not receive Capt. Halleck's letter for some time, as, even if the steamer stops at San Pedro, I will probably be gone, & there is not much communication between this place & that.

Our map is finished & is a very pretty one.[117] Temple & Riquena,[118] the two *comisionados*, have to see that the stones are

[116]Lt. John Hamilton (1823-1900), 3d artillery.

[117]The original map is preserved in the archives of the city clerk of Los Angeles. The size is 28½ x 30½ inches. A reduced reproduction, accompanied by a sketch of Lt. Ord by J. Gregg Layne, was published in Hist. Soc. of Sou. Calif. *Quarterly Publication*, XVII, 139-42. See also W. W. Robinson, "Story of Ord's Survey as Disclosed by the Los Angeles Archives," *ibid.*, XIX, 121-31.

[118]Manuel Requena (1804?-76), alcalde of Los Angeles in 1836, and several times a member of the city council. (Bancroft, V, 691-92.)

all down at the corners of the squares, & then it will be delivered. We will probably start Monday (the 3d).

There is plenty of work, in the neighborhood of this place, which ought to be done, if the people only thought so. Temple has a lien on the San Pedro ranch (Domingues') &, if he can get the part he wants, intends to lay out a town immediately; but he will not be able to do anything for several months yet.

My "connexion with O.," of which you speak, will soon be over now, and I would rather, by far, do anything with or for Mr. Halleck than with anybody else I know. What is he going to do, now that he has taken such a big house? When I first arrived I heard some person (Mr. Wilson, I believe) "expect he was going to run for governor," & "think he would be the best they could get," but the people generally do not look so far ahead, & those who troubled themselves with thinking of public matters, took more interest in the election of delegates to the convention. It is generally supposed at the north that Frémont is very popular here, but that does not seem to be the case. *They say* he gave rowdy balls & so became popular with the lower classes, but the best families *could* not attend them & consequently were not influenced by them. As to his having a fine house here,[119] he intended to engage Williams's (the old dragoons barracks), which, as Mr. Wilson says, will be in fine order when Frémont comes down, but, unfortunately for him, it will have another owner, Wilson himself having bought [it] to fit up as a billiard & eating house.[120]

Mr. Prior has had several attacks of his disease, lately, and has

[119]Frémont actually resided in Los Angeles only from Jan. until May, 1847.

[120]The old adobe building, formerly owned by Isaac Williams, was the official residence of Gov. Pico at the time of the American occupation. It was used for housing federal troops until May, 1849, when it was bought by Benjamin D. Wilson. In 1850 it became the first courthouse of Los Angeles County, and in 1851 the Bella Union Hotel. Later the old structure became part of the St. Charles Hotel, which was finally torn down, in 1940.

gone down to San Pedro, to try salt water bathing, which has done him much good before this. Dr. Griffin thought he had *ossification of the valves of the heart* but Dr. Hope thinks it simply a nervous disease & which may be cured.

Frank Mellus[121] is established in business here. Bell has retired. Wilson's store is in the old place[122] but he has moved his family to the volunteer barracks, which have been put in very good order, and it is a very nice house. The books I leave in Temple's store; I did not intend to buy unless you advised it. I have written to Jim & also to Jim Overstreet, but the letters have not gone yet.

I frequently wish to be in Monterey, were it only to keep you company; any company is sometimes better than none, & I know the Colonel must be occupied at home, &, as to Capt. Halleck, he is always busy. I don't think I would have left you so soon if I had known you would remain on duty any length of time.

Dr. Golden,[123] a celebrated surgical instrument maker from New York, has arrived here. He says that Lt. Pleasanton[124] is on his way to this country, by the Spanish Trail, with a few dra-

[121]Francis Mellus (1824-63) came to California in 1839. He was a partner, with his brother Henry, in the firm of Mellus, Howard & Co., of San Francisco, and came to Los Angeles, where, associated with David W. Alexander, he conducted the southern branch of the firm. (Harris Newmark, *Sixty Years in Southern California* [3d ed.; Boston, 1930], pp. 61-62.)

[122]"In 1849 Wilson & Packard, whose store was on Main street, where the Farmers' & Merchants' Bank now stands, were the custodians of the letters for Los Angeles." (James M. Guinn, *Historical and Biographical Record of Los Angeles* [Chicago, 1901], p. 121.)

[123]William R. Golding is listed in *Doggett's New York City Directory for 1850-1851* as a surgical-instrument maker. Nothing has been found concerning his visit to Los Angeles, other than Hutton's statement.

[124]Alfred Pleasonton (1824-97), second lieutenant of 2d regiment, U.S. dragoons. While in Santa Fé in the spring of 1849, he was appointed assistant adjutant general on the staff of Gen. Persifor F. Smith, and marched with a small command of dragoons from Santa Fé to San Francisco. He attained eminence as a cavalry commander during the Civil War. (*House Report, No. 340, 50th Congress, 1st Session* [Washington, 1888].)

goons, & Carson as his guide, having left Santa Fé the 1' of June. This has since been contradicted by persons who saw Kit, in June, in New Mexico, & if he had started he would have been in long before this. Dr. Lewis Edwards[125] is in Santa Fé. Major Weightman[126] is paymaster, but very sick when they left. Reports are brought in, every day more certain, of a robbery committed at Cienagua, I believe in Sonora, by a party of Americans headed by a Dr. Lemon well known to many in this country as a remarkably smart & bad man. They hung the priest & cut him down, to make him tell where the church plate was secreted—also his brother, but neglected the cutting-down part of the operation; they sacked the convent, committed all kinds of outrages.[127] Several persons passing offered for sale pieces of plate, in Wilson's store & others. It is said Shoto was one of the crowd. His name was in a list of the party who left New Mexico, forwarded by Col. Washington,[128] but there is no proof of his being there, though he arrived in this country at the same time as the rest of the party. The Indians are troublesome at the crossing of the Colorado.

We had our horses sent in, yesterday, from Lugo's ranch.[129] The old Frenchman at Prior's put them in the corral & went off to find a stick to fasten the door; but they took advantage of

[125]Dr. Lewis A. Edwards, assistant surgeon, U.S. army, stationed at Santa Fé.

[126]Richard Hanson Weightman (1816-61), an additional paymaster of volunteers and a captain in Clark's battalion of Missouri volunteers in the war with Mexico. He edited a newspaper in Santa Fé and was a delegate to the 32d Congress, 1851-53.

[127]Probably refers to the attack on Cieneguita, in the district of Altar, northern Sonora, by California emigrants, mentioned in *Informe de la comision pesquisidora de la frontera del Noroeste* (México, 1875), pp. 7-8 (not seen). (Rufus K. Wyllys, *The French in Sonora (1850-1854)* [Berkeley, 1932], p. 50.)

[128]Lt. Col. John Macrae Washington (1797-1853), governor of New Mexico, Oct., 1848-Oct., 1849.

[129]Doubtless the Rancho San Antonio of Antonio María Lugo, lying southeast of the pueblo.

his absence, to walk out into the vineyard, & the old woman forthwith ordered them to be turned out. We recovered them this morning, as they went straight back to the ranch.

I pass my time as agreeably as could be expected in this place. I have been to see Mrs. Stearns two or three times, & that is the amount of my visiting. Night before last I was there & met the Rose (as she is called) of California,[130] a very pretty young lady &, from appearances & report, as good as she is pretty. Mr. Wilson is my principal society & I like him very much—a quiet, kind man, who has spent much of his life in the mountains & has done a great deal for us. I am coming to the end of my sheet & must stop now. Give my best respects to the Major & Mrs. Canby, con expresiones y mil gracias to the Doña for her kindness. My best regards to Capt. Halleck, from whom I hope to hear soon, & to the Colonel, & expresiones a todas.

. . . .

The old hospital steward, French, & his party have come down & intend to reside here. They are considered very honest, good men, having only committed perjury & robbed both Uncle Sam & private individuals.

[Addressed:] Major William Rich, A. Pmr., U.S.A.
Monterey, Calfa.
[Corrected to read:] Washington City, D.C.

Letters, 1850

Monterey, Jany. 31, 1850.

My dear Mother,

I received your kind letter of Dec. 10, with its enclosure for Jim, the day after he left here for San Miguel, where he has gone to purchase cattle to drive up to San Francisco. I will send your letter by Jim Overstreet, who is still here, sleeping on the

130The identity of this young woman has not been discovered.

floor in my little room, which just holds us both. Jim was very anxious to have seen Uncle before he went, & says he came down here on purpose to see me. When our Jim was here I talked to him about going home; he would not think of it—says he will probably go to Mexico soon, &c.

I am pretty well and getting along as well as usual. Doña Angustias sends you many thanks for your kindness in offering to take care of her boys;[131] she has been pretty sick, but is now much better. Mr. Sully (of Philadelphia)[132] has painted for her an original historical piece, but has not yet been able to send it.

. . . .

We have no church here yet, and I occasionally get a good many hits about bigotry, illiberality, and the like. . . .

We have a very wet winter. Sacramento city is 6 or 8 feet under water, & Vernon [footnote: At the junction of Feather & Sacramento rivers] & the others up the river are *nowhere.*

. . . .

To Ellen S. Hutton

Monterey, Cal., April 15/50.

My dear Sister:

I write in order that a mail may not go without something from me, in case a steamer comes down tomorrow. I have very little news—none, I may say. . . . I have had an offer (as yet I have not answered it) to go to San Luis Obispo to

[131]Antonio and Porfirio Jimeno Casarin, who accompanied Capt. William T. Sherman east in Jan., 1850, and entered Georgetown College. (Sherman, *Memoirs,* I, 109.)

[132]The artist Thomas Sully (1783-1872), whose son, Capt. Alfred Sully (1821-79), married Manuelita Jimeno Casarin, of Monterey. See Hutton's letter of Sept. 30, 1850. In 1851 Thomas Sully painted, from daguerreotypes, heads of Alfred and Manuelita, and at an unknown date two miniatures of the latter. (Edward Biddle and Mantle Fielding, *The Life and Works of Thomas Sully* [Philadelphia, 1921], pp. 284, 331.) The "historical piece" mentioned by Hutton is not included in the list of Sully's paintings which appears in that volume.

survey a good deal of land there at a monthly pay. I think I shall do it, but we have not talked about the price yet.

Tell Uncle that Padre Ramirez[133] is well and sends memorias—Capt. Burton, the same. Halleck is expected down in a day or two. Manuelita and Teresita[134] are in from the farm and as amiable as [ever]. I believe I would fall in love with Teresita if she were not engaged. . . .

. . . .

Tell Uncle Gen. Smith has gone to San Diego, to come up by land, & probably Gen. Riley will not go. Lt. Derby, escorted by Moore's company of infantry, has started for Lake Buenavista (Tulares).[135] An expedition is being organized against the Indians of Clear Lake, north of Sonoma.[136] Maj. Seawell commands, & Wescott's, Wessell's (infy.), & Davidson's (dragoon) companies compose the command.

[133] Padre Ignacio Ramírez de Arrellano, who had been vice-president of the missions of Lower California in 1847, arrived in Monterey in 1849 and remained there as parish priest until Feb., 1853, when he was recalled to Mexico. He was one of the chaplains of the constitutional convention of 1849. (Zephyrin Engelhardt, *The Missions and Missionaries of California: Upper California*, IV [San Francisco, 1915], *passim; ibid., Lower California*, I [2d ed.; Santa Barbara, 1929], pp. 670, 679.)

[134] Manuelita Jimeno Casarin and her cousin, Teresita Hartnell.

[135] Lt. George H. Derby's report of this expedition, dated Monterey, July 10, 1850, was printed in Washington, 1852, with the title, *Report of the Secretary of War, Communicating, . . . a Report of the Tulare Valley* (32d Cong., 1st Sess.; Senate Ex. Doc. No. 110).

[136] An expedition sent to punish a tribe of Pomo Indians for the killing of two white settlers in the fall of 1849. Maj. Washington Seawell, at first assigned to command the expedition, having been ordered to Oregon was succeeded by Lt. Nathaniel Lyon. Lyon's report, dated Anderson's Rancho, May 22, 1850, is printed in Millard Fillmore, *Message of the President . . . December 2, 1850* (31st Cong., 2d Sess.; Senate Ex. Doc. No. 1; Washington, 1850), Pt. II, pp. 81-83.

To Nathaniel Henry Hutton

Monterey, April 18, 1850.

Dear Bud:

I have not written to you for such a long time that now, while I have time, I will give you a letter. There has been a continual change in affairs in this country. The legislature is almost entirely composed of rowdies, kicking up a fuss all the time. They are disgusted with San José as the capital of the state, but cannot agree upon a place to change it to.

Business in San Francisco has been better than was expected. There have been only three failures. Frank Ward,[137] who shot himself in the head about two or three weeks ago, will probably recover. He has spoiled one eye, and the ball is still in his nose.

Five or six steamers leave San Francisco every afternoon at 4 o'clock. They say it looks like home. There are immense numbers of steamers on the bay & rivers. Steamers now run up the Sacramento 230 miles above Sacramento city, where there were a dozen houses last year at this time, and the city now contains 15,000 inhabitants. Stockton, which had then but one house and a number of tents, now has a population of 10,000, and there are steamers running much higher up the San Joaquin River; there are four or five cities, some of them thriving ones, above it. Vernon,[138] Fremont,[139] Oro,[140] Marysville, Kear-

[137]Although not a Mormon, Frank Ward came to San Francisco with Samuel Brannan, on the "Brooklyn," in July, 1846. He was a member of the mercantile firm of Ward & Smith, and held several official positions in San Francisco. The death of his young bride, and business losses, led to his attempted suicide. (Bancroft, V, 766-67.)

[138]Founded, in 1849, on the east bank of the Feather River, at its junction with the Sacramento, Vernon flourished for several years, and in 1851 was the county seat of Sutter County. No trace of it remains today.

[139]Fremont, started in 1849 across the Sacramento River from Vernon, was the county seat of Yolo County in 1850-51. This town, too, has disappeared.

[140]Oro was laid out, on paper, on the south bank of the Bear River, by Thomas J. Green, a state senator. Through his influence it became the first county seat of Sutter County, but was soon abandoned.

ny,[141] Yuba,[142] Plumas,[143] & Linda,[144] are on the Sacramento & its branches.

Gold has been found in small quantities in the "Coyote"[145] at San José, and *in the large ravine at Monterey*. Tell Uncle this; he always said so.

Ellen's favorite musician, *Herz*,[146] has been performing in San Francisco, and I am told to as decent looking audiences as could be seen in New York.

. . . .

April 23d.

The steamer came in day before yesterday but I only recd. one letter from Mother, dated March 11'. I have none for February. The new steamers, Tennessee[147] & Gold Hunter,[148]

141This was a town projected on Johnson's rancho, at the crossing of Bear River, near Camp Far West. It "never progressed to any extent beyond the laying out of the lots." (William H. Chamberlain, *History of Yuba County* [Oakland, 1879], p. 78.)

142The present Yuba City, county seat of Sutter County.

143Plumas was laid out, in the spring of 1850, by John A. Sutter and George H. Beach, on Feather River, just below the mouth of Reed's Dry Creek. A hotel was the only building erected. (Chamberlain, *op. cit.*, p. 79.)

144This town was also started in the spring of 1850, on the south bank of the Yuba River, nearly opposite Marysville. A few houses were built, but the place was abandoned two years later. (*Ibid.*, pp. 75-76.)

145Coyote Creek, Santa Clara County.

146Henri Herz (1806-88), a Viennese pianist, toured the United States (including California), Mexico, and the West Indies, from 1845 to 1851. (George R. MacMinn, *The Theater of the Golden Era in California* [Caldwell, Idaho, 1941], pp. 366-69.)

147A side-wheeler, built in New York and purchased by the Pacific Mail Steamship Company. She arrived in San Francisco, on her first trip, on Apr. 14, 1850. (Ernest A. Wiltsee, *Gold Rush Steamers* [San Francisco, 1938], p. 24.)

148The "Gold Hunter," 436 tons, arrived in San Francisco, from New York, Apr. 28, 1850. She plied at first between San Francisco and Sacramento. (San Francisco *Daily Pacific News*, Apr. 30, 1850.)

and, I believe, the Sarah Sands,[149] have arrived, and the Tennessee has gone down again.

The gold mines which create most excitement, now, are those on Trinity River—the more so as it is accessible by sea. We heard, yesterday, of the death of five persons at Trinity Bay, by the swamping of a boat; two were naval officers.[150] Lt. Bache and I can't find out certainly who the other was.

The mail-rider from below brought up a report that the Mormons & Texans had united, below, to drive out all other Americans, saying that the country pertained to "Deseret"[151]—this, I believe, in the neighborhood of San Luis Rey. But Genl. Smith has ordered 2 companies of cavalry to be stationed there and they will help to keep things quiet.

. . . .

Nipoma, May 24, 1850.

My dear Mother:

Although I am afraid I will not be able to get this letter to Monterey in time for the mail, yet I will at least have it ready for any opportunity that offers.

I wrote from Monterey before I left, stating my expectations. I left very unexpectedly on Monday morning, starting for San José to avoid the necessity of Mr. Tefft[152] returning to

[149]The "Sarah Sands," 1,500 tons, was built in Great Britain, and was purchased by the Empire City Line, a competitor of the Pacific Mail Company. She left New York, Dec. 10, 1849, but did not arrive in San Francisco until June 6, 1850. (*Ibid.*, p. 38.)

[150]Lts. Richard Bache and Robert L. Browning were drowned in Trinity Bay, on Mar. 27, 1850. (Bancroft, VI, 502.)

[151]In Mar., 1849, the Mormons organized the State of Deseret, elected Brigham Young governor, and applied to Congress for admission to the Union. The proposed state failed of recognition and, in Sept., 1850, an act was passed by Congress, providing for the organization of Utah Territory.

[152]Henry Amos Tefft (1824-52) was one of the delegates to the constitutional convention of 1849, and assemblyman from San Luis Obispo County in the first legislature. In 1850 he became judge of the second judicial district—a position

Monterey. The first day we went only to Alisal,[153] which is on the main road, and there left the greater part of our carriage load of baggage. The next day we went as far as Murphy's,[154] where I saw for the first time Miss Ellen Murphy,[155] of whom Uncle will tell you more. The third day, as we went into San José, about 10 o'clock, we met the funeral of the person whom Mr. Tefft expected to take home in his carriage. We were obliged to remain two days in S. José, to have the carriage fixed and the horses and mules shod, and to fix a new set of harness to drive four horses in the carriage. The first day, we reached San Juan, over a very bad road; the second, we stopped at the Alisal to take "on board" our freight, and then, driving on, passed the house where we intended to stop, without seeing it, & camped about five miles from Soledad[156]—a very long day's drive. The next day passed Soledad and continued on, 12 or 15 miles, to La Poza,[157] where we breakfasted. In the evening, after passing another rancho (which, as well as La Poza, having been deserted on account of the Indians, were now being re-established), we arrived at Ojitos,[158] but were

---

which he held until his death, by drowning, at Port Harford, near San Luis Obispo, on Feb. 6, 1852. (*Alta California*, Steamer ed., Feb. 18, 1852.) In July, 1850, Tefft married, at Nipomo Rancho, María Josefa, eldest daughter of William G. Dana. Hutton attended the wedding and left a description of it in manuscript.

[153]There were two ranches of this name in Monterey County, both granted in 1834—one to Feliciano and Mariano Soberanes, the other to William E. P. Hartnell.

[154]Martin Murphy's Rancho Ojo de Agua de la Coche, in Santa Clara County.

[155]Ellen Murphy, daughter of Martin, came with her father to California, in 1844, and in 1850 married Charles Maria Weber, founder of Stockton. (Bancroft, IV, 749.)

[156]Soledad Mission, some thirty miles southeast of Monterey.

[157]Rancho Poza de los Ositos, in Monterey County, granted in 1839 to Carlos Cayetano Espinosa.

[158]Rancho Los Ojitos, lying along the San Antonio River, granted in 1842 to Mariano Soberanes.

so churlishly received that we went on half a mile and camped. He[re] the provisions which Doña Angustias had put up for me was reduced to a very small piece of musty bread, and, as we had nothing the next morning but some milk we found at a house by the road-side, we felt rather wolfish at night, when, after passing San Miguel[159] and driving thence over a beautiful country, we reached El Paso de Robles.[160] Here they gave us an excellent supper, and we slept, from choice, in the carriage. From this place a good cart road passes into the Tulare Valley, through which supplies will undoubtedly be sent to the southern mines. The next day we reached Santa Margarita[161] by breakfast time, but would not stop. This is one of the most beautiful spots in California—well watered plains, and slopes with groves of oak and pine woods. From this the road is bad for a carriage, and we had a hard time going the next ten miles, to S. Luis, but it is a beautiful country, with dashing streams of clear water and with gravelly bottoms at every half mile or less. I found no person at S. Luis who could start to [i.e., me] in my work there, and, by Mr. Tefft's advice, I left all my things there and went on with him to see Mr. Price,[162] some 12 miles farther on. We passed, with much difficulty (on account of gullies), over a beautiful country, one spot of which has attracted the attention of everyone who has seen it, as the best spot for cultivation in the country. As Mr. Price was not at home I was obliged

[159]San Miguel Mission, in northern San Luis Obispo County.

[160]Rancho Paso de Robles, originally belonging to San Miguel Mission, but granted in 1844 to Pedro Narváez.

[161]Rancho Santa Margarita formerly belonged to San Luis Obispo Mission, but was granted in 1841 to Joaquín Estrada.

[162]John Michael Price (1810-1902) came to Monterey in 1830, and to San Luis Obispo in 1836. He was owner of the Pismo Rancho, 7,000 acres, which Hutton probably hoped to survey. (Annie L. Morrison and John H. Haydon, *History of San Luis Obispo County* [Los Angeles, 1917], pp. 52-53.)

to go on to Nipoma[163] with Mr. Tefft, and after crossing the 'arroyo grande,' a very miry, half-bridged stream, and going up a hill it [i.e., we] thought we could not get up, we had a very pleasant drive to this place. I found Capt. Dana[164] an excellent, good natured old gentleman, and his daughter is a favorite with all who know her—among others, of Uncle. Since I have been here they have treated me very kindly, and they live very comfortably. I sent up to San Luis for my things, and have commenced on this farm, as I cannot well do anything in S. Luis until Capt. Wilson[165] comes down. The farm is about 10 miles long and, I believe, nearly as many broad, though a third of it is hilly and good for nothing. The air is filled with the fragrance of the different species of clover, and in some places the oats are 4 feet high.

They have about thirty or forty tame cows, and we have lots of milk and fresh butter.

I am very impatiently awaiting the arrival of a vessel from Monterey, with the rest of my clothes and instruments, more especially a 'transit compass' which I have purchased from Mr. Bestor[166] for $250—the cost of the instrument ($140) and some drawing "fixins," with the transportation ($75).

[163]Rancho Nipoma (or Nipomo), nearly 38,000 acres, granted to Capt. William G. Dana in 1837.

[164]William Goodwin Dana (1797-1858) was born in Boston and settled in Santa Barbara in 1825, after having been engaged in trading voyages, for several years, from Boston to China, the Hawaiian Islands, and California. He was a cousin of Richard Henry Dana, author of *Two Years Before the Mast.* (Helen S. Giffen, "An Adopted Californian," in Hist. Soc. of Sou. Calif. *Quarterly*, XIX, 49-62.)

[165]John Wilson (1795-1860), Scotch shipmaster and trader, who came to California in 1826. He was the owner, with his partner James Scott, of the ranchos Cañada de los Osos and Cañada del Chorro, in San Luis Obispo County. (Bancroft, V, 777.)

[166]Probably Norman S. Bestor, who came to California in 1846 as assistant to Lt. William H. Emory. (Bancroft, V, 337.) He was associated with Lts. William T. Sherman and William H. Warner, in a store at Coloma, in the winter of 1848-49, and is mentioned in Sherman's *Memoirs.*

I have made my arrangements to survey this farm at $300 per month, all my assistants and expenses being furnished, but I do not think I will do any more for less than $400, as it will not be so constant as I had anticipated. A county surveyor has been chosen in Santa Barbara,[167] but I suspect the same way as in this county—a man who does not want nor is capable of filling the office, to which he was elected because he was popular and there was no other office for him. I did expect, & do still, to have the survey of Sta. Barbara, unless they should do as the Montereyans did—have a map made so entirely incorrect that it has done more harm than good. I could easily be appointed surveyor for this county, but I would not work for the pay, which is very small.

The numbers of Sonorians that pass up the country, on their way to the mines, are astonishing. It is said the Indians are very troublesome there, and some think that the greater number of the inhabitants will come to this country. Indeed, it must be very populous if many are left now. Those whom I have met say that they will not pay the $20 monthly, for permission to work in the mines, which the legislature has imposed on all foreigners.[168] The people in the lower part of the country say that they will not pay their taxes, but I expect they don't think that they can easily be made to do so. There is a great ignorance of law and government among the lower classes, and they have been accustomed to have everything their own way—but times are changing with them.

I suppose you will see in the papers the news of the fire in San Francisco.

[167]The name of the earliest county surveyor appearing in the county records is Vitus Wackenreuder, who held the office in 1852-53. (Letter from O. H. O'Neill, county surveyor, Aug. 26, 1940.)

[168]This foreign miners' tax, imposed by the legislature in 1850, was found to be excessive and was repealed the next year. In 1852 the tax was fixed at $3 monthly, and in 1853 at $4.

I thought that extravagant prices had commenced passing away, but had to pay $7 per day at the hotel in S. José, and, worse yet, $2 for a meal of milk and (miscalled) tea, on the road.

I have found here several good books to read—among others, Moratin's Comedies and, best of all, Keble's Christian Year. . . .

. . . .

Monterey, Sept. 30', 1850.

Dear Mother,

You see I am back again in Monterey. I came for the purpose of finding that *box,* but as Capt. Burton is on a court martial in San Diego I have not succeeded as yet. I have written to Halleck but have no answer yet. Please find out & let me know the name of the Californian agent of Lount & Co.'s express[169] & send me one of the bills of lading or receipts, if you have them, tho' I hope to have the box long before I receive them. If I should not I may need them. I was some days in San Luis doing nothing, waiting for a chance to come up, as I dislike travelling alone. I left in company with a Mr. Beebee,[170] & the first day we only travelled 25 miles, to "Paso de Robles," stopping on the road at Santa Margarita. The next day we were off at daylight, without any breakfast and in a rain storm (which, however, was not very severe), and, after riding over a beautiful rolling country covered with oak groves, high hills, & mountains, on one side, and, on the other, the willow-bordered river of Monterey, we reached the deserted mission of San Miguel about 8 o'clock. Here we found some Indians, with an ox they

[169]Said to have been a defaulting company, conducted by one Lount, which "ran from San Francisco through Sacramento to the mines and even attempted a service to New York." (Alvin F. Harlow, *Old Waybills* [New York, 1934], p. 117.)

[170]Probably William L. Beebee (1829-99), who came to California in Aug., 1847, on the U.S. storeship "Southampton," and settled in San Luis Obispo in 1849. He was elected justice of the peace in 1851, and county supervisor in 1852. (*History of San Luis Obispo County*, pp. 133, 135.)

had killed; and, after breakfasting on roasted ribs, we kept on down the valley of the river—a road seldom travelled. It is an excellent road, thro' a wide valley (except in one or two places where the hills come down to the river), and is said to be much shorter than the one usually travelled. Part of the road is in the bed of the river, which is very wide and full of willows, with, at this season, only a few streams of water meandering through it. My companion was afraid of tiring his horses by galloping, so we went all day at a trot, and at 4 o'clock I was so tired that I could scarcely ride. I then changed my horse and was soon quite rested. About nine o'clock at night we arrived at the Poza, a small rancho on the plain of the river, about 55 or 60 miles from Monterey, having travelled from seventy to eighty miles. We were too much fatigued to be disturbed by about seven hundred head of cattle in a corral, by which we slept, & in the morning were off again at daylight. Arriving at the Soledad,[171] breakfast was over & we stood a poor chance, when one of the girls (Francisca, an acquaintance of Uncle's) recognized me thro' the window & told her mother that I was the nephew of the "Señor Rico." She called to me at once to get off & come in, was very happy to see me, &c., as Uncle had recommended me to her when he went away, tho' I was in Los Angeles. In a very short time they had on the table a nice breakfast, &, soon after, in came the other young ladies, and they brought water-melons & cantelopes & all sorts of nice things. The old lady sent many memorias to Uncle—and also Gabriela & Carmenita. After stopping a couple of hours to chat, we went on, stopping on the road to feed the animals, & afterwards to leave some of them at Buena Vista,[172] and got into Monterey a little after dark. I did not know the place, for the

[171]The Soledad Mission lands were granted, in 1846, to Feliciano Soberanes, father of the three girls who entertained the travelers.

[172]Rancho Buena Vista, in Monterey County.

houses, when I arrived, but managed to find my way to the fort, where I am now staying. I found things very much altered here. Manuelita's marriage[173] has caused a great deal of ill-feeling. The Doña is the same as ever towards me. She has a little baby, too, but it is very sick & will hardly live long. I am glad I was not here in the wedding times, for it was done in a manner that I hardly think very creditable to many who were engaged in it, and, tho' I never have expressed an opinion with regard to it, *They say* that I said something—I don't know what—which would or might have offended Sully; but it makes no difference to me. I do not like to quarrel, nor to have any person angry with me, but, if they are so foolish as to be so, I am satisfied with knowing that I have given no cause fo[r it]. Lt. [name undeciphered] is here, now, but goes to San Diego. He told me—what you had already written—that he ha[d] been there & that you were all well.

I must stop, now, but will commence again [word missing]. The weather has been very fine and there are no s[igns] of early rains—the better for me, if I was not losing so [much] time. Tell Uncle I cannot find out anything about the [word missing] of Pickeringia.[174] I had no chance to look for it until now, & it is too late I will look for it in some herbaria which are in town, this afternoon. The P. D. [Pay Department?] flourishes but I know nothing about it. Nobody is here now. . . .

To William Rich

Monterey, Oct. 8th, 1850.

Dear Uncle,

While I am waiting here to send my things down, I will employ myself writing to you. Primeramente, I received from

[173]The marriage of Manuelita Jimeno Casarin and Capt. Alfred Sully.

[174]A wild shrub, with rose-purple flowers, growing in the coast range of California, and named for Charles Pickering, naturalist of the Wilkes exploring expedition.

San Francisco, by the same steamer that took home my *complaining letter, the box;* Major Smith[175] brought it down from San Francisco, and I can now account for its delay. The express you started it by can have no agent out here, and, having shipped the box at New York, it went to Chagres and, having no one to look after it, was left there until Nelson & Zacchrisson[176] had it carried to Panama, stored, and advertised in San Francisco. Lt. Gibbs[177] saw a package for him, advertised, and also this for Capt. Burton, and sent for both, and, as Maj. Smith was coming down, he brought this for me. I have paid the expenses from Chagres, $53—which I suppose you can recover if the express is still in existence. I send you the bill, enclosed.

The transit is a perfect beauty. Being packed on its side, the screws which fastened it to the slide drew, and it was a little bruised, but scarcely perceptibly. The compass box had fallen off & broken short the steel centre on which the needle turns, but there is in town a very fine workman who put in another for me very nicely. The glass, of course, was broken but that was of no consequence. Terry[178] has a cabinet-maker employed, who is to make me a tripod tomorrow, and then I will be all right. The instrument appears to be perfect in all its adjustments. The drawing paper is excellent and a perfect godsend. I had just got two sheets from Ord, on condition of "marking a few lines on a map the doctor[179] has," which took me half a day, but I was glad to get it at that price. The drawing instruments are very excellent ones for use, and the pencils and little things

[175]Maj. Albert J. Smith, army paymaster.

[176]Zachrisson, Nelson & Co., a firm of merchants and steamship agents at Panama.

[177]Lt. Alfred Gibbs, aide-de-camp to Maj. Gen. Persifor F. Smith.

[178]Not identified.

[179]Probably Dr. James L. Ord, brother of Lt. Ord and assistant surgeon of Company F, 3d U.S. artillery. He later married Doña Angustias, widow of Manuel Jimeno Casarin.

are a supply for years. I see you thought of mouthglue, 'tambien.' Of clothing, too, I now have enough to last me a small lifetime, and it is astonishing how well they fit. As for books, The Art Journal is the admiration of every body that sees it, and the plates are such that any two (to change occasionally) would retain for a year their power of pleasing. I have read two or three chapters, only, in Lazarillo but it seems to merit its reputation. . . .

For news about town, there is scarcely any. Dr. Randall[180] is, I believe, elected to the assembly. This is all the politics.

Mr. and Mrs. Sully seem to get on very well. They live in Halleck's old house, which is quite nicely fixed up. They have very few visits from the "gente del pais." They say they can tell by their visitors when there is a prospect of reconciliation—that when such is the case people begin to come, but as soon as the prospect changes they are deserted. I expect it will be made up soon, tho' the Doña has never said a word to me about it. As the house is a little out of sight and I have been quite busy, I had only been to the house once, when Hamilton[181] told me that they (Mr. and Mrs. Sully) thought I staid away for fear of offending the Señora. But I told him it was not & was nonsense to think so—that I would not be much affected by her opinion in doing what I thought was right. But I think the reverse is actually the case—that pride is the only difficulty

[180]Dr. Andrew Randall, a Kentuckian, elected a member of the second California assembly, and later a claimant for large tracts of land in Butte, Marin, and Monterey counties. He died in San Francisco on July 26, 1856, the victim of an attack by Joseph Hetherington, whom the Committee of Vigilance executed for the crime. Bancroft confuses Dr. Randall with Andrew A. Randall, gunner on the U.S. vessel "Portsmouth," who came to California in 1847 and died in 1865. (San Francisco *Daily Evening Bulletin,* July 25-28, 1856; Ogden Hoffman, *Reports of Land Cases* [San Francisco, 1862]; Edward W. Callahan, *List of Officers of the Navy of the United States* [New York, 1901], p. 451.)

[181]Lt. John Hamilton.

she has to overcome and that she would appreciate any attention showed Manuelita, so that she were not implicated.

I mentioned in some of my letters* —— as being common about San Luis. I said this, having only seen the plant while riding by and being ignorant of the family of . [Marginal note: * I cannot, for my life, recollect the name of this—bears a loose spike of bright scarlet flowers, long & tubular. A specimen (of which I made a drawing in [?] Darwin) is in the house.] Mr. Laub,[182] a Scotch collector now here, calls it a penstemon. It is bright scarlet, and very large. He (Mr. L. [)] went to San Antonio[183] & Los Ojitos, looking for Pinus Sinclairii, which I had told him was found there. He says I was mistaken—it is Sabinianus;[184] but he found Sinclairii higher up, on the mountains of Santa Lucia—and also Benthamianus.[185] The second species which you noticed at this place is P. Edgarianus.[186] He says that the origin of the name of P. Sinclairii is unknown, *that Sir W. J. Hooker told him so*, and that in speaking of it in his communications he mentioned it as being yours; but if I am not mistaken it is Sir William's own.[187] I think I recollect the figure in Beechy. Mr. L. has also what he thinks a new oak, but knows nothing of a laurel-leaved oak which I

182 Probably William Lobb, a botanist and collector, who came to California in 1849, as representative of a large English nursery. He sent to England many seeds of western trees, including the first to reach there of the recently discovered big trees of the Calaveras grove. Lobb remained in California, and died in San Francisco in 1863. (Alice Eastwood, "Early Botanical Explorers on the Pacific Coast," in Calif. Hist. Soc. *Quarterly*, XVIII, 343.)

183 Mission San Antonio de Padua, near Jolon, in Monterey County.

184 *Pinus Sabiniana Douglas,* commonly known as the gray (or digger) pine. (George B. Sudworth, *Forest Trees of the Pacific Slope* [Washington, 1908], pp. 54-56.)

185 An early name given to *Pinus ponderosa Lawson,* or western yellow pine. (Jackson, *Index Kewensis,* III, 530.)

186 *Pinus Edgariana,* now known as *Pinus muricata Don* (pricklecone, or bishop's, pine). (*Ibid.,* pp. 531-32; Sudworth, *op. cit.,* pp. 65-68.)

187 See above, n. 49.

think you have, and which from all I can learn is very abundant in the pass in the mountains near El Paso de Robles, south of San Miguel, and is spoken of as equal to any imported wood for hardness and durability. I want to get specimens if I can and send them to you. I will recollect tomorrow and ask the Indian names of the redwood—and put them in.

. . . .

Monterey, Oct. 9, 1850.

My dear Mother,

As you will see by my letter of yesterday to Uncle, I have that box; and as I cannot thank you in words I leave it for you to imagine. I have now everything I want—books, instruments, and clothing. . . .

The tracts I have, or will, read and then distribute, if possible, but I don't know how, as Mr. Willey[188] had an immense number of tracts and could not get rid of them; and a number of prayerbooks which I had, I placed in a store to be given away, or sold for almost nothing, and I see they are still there.

. . . .

The instrument is a very fine one and I have it all fixed, now, as good as ever, and the chain the very thing I want. I have been using a fifty foot chain (and that borrowed), and it is only convenient in surveying a town.

. . . .

I did not say anything to Uncle about the Padre.[189] He is

[188]Samuel Hopkins Willey (1821-1914), sent to California by the American Home Missionary Society, arrived at Monterey on Feb. 23, 1849. He was the first Protestant clergyman to hold services there, and alternated with Padre Ramírez de Arrellano as a chaplain of the constitutional convention. In May, 1850, he removed to San Francisco and became pastor of the Howard Presbyterian Church. He was active in the organization of the College of California, afterward the University of California, and was successively its vice-president and acting president.

[189]See above, n. 133.

in a singular position here, at present, being president of the missions of Lower California but unable to return, either through fear of the people or for want of funds. He is not popular, here, because he talks too plainly to the people. Many of them think him heretical. His sermon on Sunday morning was on the abuse of the Sacraments. "Many persons," he says, "to save the trouble of repenting as often as they sin, leave the Sacraments until their last hour, in order to do away at one blow with all their offences." This is what he calls "the blasphemy of laying a trap for God." . . . These and other doctrines, such as the sinfulness of giving divine honors to the saints, &c., have brought him into great disrepute. He is thinking seriously of going to the Atlantic States.

. . . .

I put in some little sketches which Uncle left, & have some others to send when they are finished. I have a thousand dollars here *put away*, and 6 or 700 due me in San Luis. I would invest it at 5 or 6, or perhaps 8 or 10, per cent a month, if I was where I could watch it, but there is so much rascality that I will not trust everybody. . . . This is beside the lots in San José.

. . . .

To William Rich

San Luis Obispo, Dec. 23d, 1850.

Dear Uncle,

I received, a week or two ago, your kind letter dated in Septr., with others from Ellen and Mother. I suppose you have, long before this, received my letter acknowledging the receipt of "the box," and that it had cost me $53.00 for freight. There was in it everything I could have asked for if I had made a list of my wants. The clothes all fit me remarkably well, except that the pantaloons are mostly too large, which is a fault on the right side. The instrument is a splendid one—only, too good to take into the field. At first I thought something was the matter with the needle, that it would not traverse freely, but, by leaving it free fifteen minutes before using it, it works so well that, in work where extreme accuracy was not so much sought for as to save time, I used the needle alone, without the graduated plate. I have surveyed, for Wilson, the farm and garden of the Chorro[190] (a beautiful place for a garden and dairy), and two others adjoining it, and as the rains have now commenced I am going north to attend to matters there. Bestor offered to act as my agent in paying taxes, &c., on my lots in San José, but knowing he was very short of money I sent him a note of $100, state scrip,[191] which was very nearly due. He did not receive the letter until after the lots had been sold and then, by law, they could only be redeemed by paying 100 per cent on the taxes; this, with the loss in disposing of the note for $75, which I supposed to be $100, [marginal note: It only cost me $90.] makes my lots cost me, this year, $170 or $180. Bestor has, however, taken a great deal of trouble to have the matter put straight, and my titles are now better than ever. I am going up to S. José to settle with him and see if I can sell my lots, in a week or ten days. I have two horses, now, or, rather, a mare and a horse, the latter a beautiful little yellow bay, pacer, and good for a lady to pasear or a vaquero to lazo a steer. I expected to get a fine one from Cantua[192] (whose

[190]Rancho Cañada del Chorro, in San Luis Obispo County, granted in 1845 to James Scott and John Wilson. The other tracts surveyed were presumably the Cañada de los Osos and the Huerta de Romualdo.

[191]A temporary state-loan act, approved Jan. 5, 1850, authorized the state treasurer to issue bonds, in denominations of $100, $225, $500, and $1,000, payable within six months, with interest at the rate of 3 per cent a month. These bonds were receivable for all taxes and state dues. The state revenue act, approved Mar. 30, 1850, provided, in case property was sold for taxes, for payment by the owner, when redeeming the property, of 100 per cent indemnity to the purchaser.

[192]Guadalupe Cantua, owner of Rancho San Luisito, near the Cañada del Chorro. (Bancroft, II, 741.)

farm I have surveyed), as he was short of funds, but all, except one, of his saddle horses were stolen a few days after I left.

The cholera has been at work here quite fiercely. In about two weeks it carried off more than thirty of a population of less than a hundred. Capt. Wilson's family have nearly all been sick—he himself dangerously so—but they are now nearly all well. I have been out there for a week, helping to take care of the sick ones.

I was very much disappointed in Capt. W.'s family, upon becoming more intimately acquainted with them. You know Don Juan; Doña Ramona[193] is unexceptionable, and the younger of the Pachecos; the rest give a very favorable impression at first acquaintance, but it does not bear examination; the girls are still quite young and if they could see good society they would improve.

With Mrs. Tefft [marginal note: Capt. Dana's daughter.] the case is different. I know that you think a great deal of her, & think that you would like her much more if you knew her better. That in which she most differs from her "paisanas" is in her love for reading. Altho' she has had but few books, she knows them by heart—among others, Moratin's Comedies and "Poesias sueltas."

I am delayed, at present, waiting for my pay for surveying the town here—$627—and one or two other debts, which I do not expect to have trouble in collecting.

I enclose my accounts for subsistence while traveling; as I have no data to fill them up I send them blank.[194]

[193]Capt. John Wilson (see above, n. 165) married Ramona Carrillo de Pacheco, widow of Romualdo Pacheco. She had two sons by her first marriage, one of whom became acting governor of California in 1875. (Bancroft, IV, 764.)

[194]These accounts, which have been preserved by Hutton's daughters, claim subsistence at 75 cents per day for 447 days, as follows: June 26-Aug. 11, 1847, Monterey to Los Angeles and return; Sept. 22-Oct. 12, 1847, Monterey to San Francisco and return; Oct. 22, 1847-May 12, 1848, Monterey to La Paz, Lower

I have not had much time for sketching, but I must confess that I have not employed what I have had, as I used to do. I have a few sketches, however, but I want to finish them, if possible, before sending them. Among flowers I have done nothing. I have a few specimens which I did not recognize but, having no books, I could not be certain about them. I feel some inclination to take up the trees, if I had paid any attention to them formerly, but I cannot get a start now.

I have not heard from Monterey for some time. D. Pablo de la Guerra[195] is appointed marshall & has resigned his seat in the state senate.

There is nothing more new to say . . .

You will see that I have left the letter, accompanying my accts., without direction, as I do not know to whom you present the document. . . .

[Addressed:] Maj. Wm. Rich, Washington, D.C.

[Postmarked:] Monterey Apr 2

Letters, 1851

To William Rich

Monterey, Feby. 24, 1851.

My dear Uncle,

I have just received your interesting letter of 9th ulto., and will answer it before saying anything else. You mention Viola chrysantha.[196] The collector has found it in the Sierra Nevada

California, and return; June 30-Aug. 28, 1848, Monterey to Los Angeles and San Francisco and return; Aug. 31-Oct. 17, 1848, Monterey to Los Angeles and return; Mar. 17-May 22, 1849, Monterey to "Sutters & Far West (Ft. Kearny)" and return.

[195]Pablo de la Guerra (1819-74), of Santa Barbara, a politician prominent both before and after the American occupation. Besides serving for several terms as state senator, he was a U.S. marshal, district judge, and acting lieutenant-governor. (Bancroft, III, 769.)

[196]Cut-leaf violet. (Willis L. Jepson, *Manual of the Flowering Plants of California* [Berkeley, 1923-25], pp. 643-44.)

and says that, since sending home seed, he has heard of its safe arrival. His questions to me about Pinus Sinclairii related to the origin of the name—who it was given by. Cantua was the name that puzzled me so. I recollect very distinctly the family of Chrysobalana.[197] What mountains is *Fremontia*[198] found in? I should be much pleased to hear from Spencer Baird,[199] and will do what I can for him or the Smithsonian Inst.; but you know how I am running about. I do not know whether I would be long enough in one place to do anything worth knowing, but, if he will tell me what he wants, I will do what I can and will try and collect immediately that I can get spirits to put my specimens in. Any synopses of genera or families, animal or vegetable (not mineral), that can be easily had, please send, and, if you can, send a loose plate or two of those beautiful col. ones by the Smithsonian Inst. I have forgotten almost all my natural history, for want of something to keep it in my head. I was in hopes to find some seed of Antigonon,[200] and make the drawings you want, but have sent it all home, I believe. I hav'n't forgotten Pickeringia yet, but it is too early for it now. I saw that purple Claytonia[201] in flower about a week ago (I forget its specific name), and the Dodecatheon[202] and —— ? (another name I can't remember—the umbelliferous yellow-flower sal[a]d-plant), with Draba,[203] are the only flowers out yet. We have scarcely had any rain—only three or four

[197]An ornamental shrub found in the southern states, but apparently not in California.

[198]The Californian slippery elm, named for its discoverer, John C. Frémont.

[199]Spencer Fullerton Baird (1823-88), assistant secretary of the Smithsonian Institution, 1850-78, and its secretary from 1878.

[200]A showy-flowered climber, abundant in the southern states, but not listed in Jepson's *Manual*.

[201]Also called Montia. A genus of low herbs of the purslane family.

[202]Commonly called shooting star, wild cyclamen, or mad violet.

[203]Popular name, whitlow grass. A low herb of the mustard family.

showers in all the winter, &, for this, the vegetation is so backward. Speaking of fish—I have seen more trout, this year, than ever, but there are none here nearer than Carmelo. I don't know the species.

. . . .

If you know of any tolerably good situation which I could certainly get if I should go home, I will go "right straight," because things are changed in California, so that I can't much more than make a comfortable support, and that would be better there than here. . . .

Monterey is at present the dullest place I ever was in. Nobody is here except the Doña's family (of my acquaintance, that is). Still, it would be very pleasant for me, if I were not conscious of the fact that, if I do not do anything, I won't get any money—which is the only thing that keeps me in California.

It astonishes me to think what a change has taken place within the last 3 years in this country. There are now ten or twelve steamers to Panama, two on the California coast, and an infinite number on the bay & rivers. The passage money from San Francisco to Sacramento (we paid, I believe, $20, and were four days) is one dollar, and performed in nine hours by two North River and Sound boats; there are others on the line. One can go anywhere (except to S. Luis) by steam—to the head waters of the San Joaquin and some distance up Sacramento and Feather rivers. Four or five steamers run to Trinidad, Gold Bluff, and other mining places on the coast, and they are talking about railroads.

Last month I went to S. José on horseback, from San Luis; thence, in stage, to S. Francisco. You couldn't know it except by the old City Hotel and Custom House,[204] which still remain.

[204]"The custom-house . . . was a new four-story brick building, and the most imposing edifice in the city. It was destroyed by fire on the 4th of May, 1851." (Frank Soulé, *Annals of San Francisco* [New York and San Francisco, 1855], p. 282.)

On the same square with the latter building are three-story buildings, and opposite the corner of the Plaza, where purser Price's[205] office was, is the St. Francis Hotel;[206] it is of wood only, but is probably by this time torn down and a large brick one commenced. The Parker House,[207] & Union Hotel[208] next to it (the first is a gambling house only), are four stories high, of brick, & the Exchange,[209] separated from the Union by a street from the middle of the Plaza, is the same size. Where Howard[210] & the other stores were are fine brick stores and large houses used by lawyers as offices. Halleck's is at the corner of this street and Commercial, a new one through the middle of the block in front of the old City Hotel. He lives in Happy Valley, the second one of those sandy valleys two miles from what used to be San Francisco. Mr. Willey lives in the first, and some most beautiful cottages are all around him. Mrs. Burton is staying with Mrs. Willey. As I had nothing to do for three or four days in S. Francisco, I went up to see Mrs. Canby, at Benicia. She enjoys rather better health than formerly and is quite comfortably situated. I spent [word not deciphered] very pleasant days and had the pleasure of doing something for her which nobody else in Monterey could or

[205]Rodman McCamley Price (1816-94), who came to California in 1846, as purser of the U.S. vessel "Cyane." He was naval agent at San Francisco in 1849, but left California in 1850. (Bancroft, IV, 784.)

[206]A four-story frame building, opened in 1849; it was the fashionable hotel of the day. It was burned in 1853. (Soulé, *op. cit.*, pp. 647-49.)

[207]This hotel, on Kearny Street, facing the Plaza, was thrice destroyed by fire, the last time on May 4, 1851. (*Ibid.*, pp. 251, 254.)

[208]"The first really substantial and elegant hotel of the city," costing, with its furnishings, $250,000. (*Ibid.*, p. 649.)

[209]The California Exchange, on the corner of Clay and Kearny Streets.

[210]The firm of Mellus & Howard was the leading one of San Francisco during the years 1846-49. It was dissolved in 1850. (Soulé, pp. 779-80.)

would. It was to find some boxes left in her charge and left by her when she went to Benicia.

. . . .

Give my love to Mother and all & remember me to old friends, especially Spencer Baird . . .

I am much obliged to Don Spencer for the name, tho (but you needn't tell him this) it goes against my principles to name after individuals unless for important scientific services.[211]

To William Rich

Arroyo Grande, May 18th, 1851.

Dear Uncle,

I have not heard anything at all since I left Monterey, and don't know how to get this into any civilized parts, but I will start it, at all events. I had a good deal of trouble to get to this place but finally succeeded. Since my arrival I have been engaged in the survey of this farm (Mr. Branch's)[212] and have just finished. It was a pretty rough job. He has intended to have surveyed another farm, beyond Santa Margarita, but we have just heard of the law for settling land titles in California and he may wait until this is decided. I have had quite a time here, occasionally. I went bear hunting once but we only saw one and

[211]Evidently an allusion to the fact that a new species of vireo, or flycatcher, discovered by Hutton at Monterey in 1847, had recently been named for him. The name of this species, *Vireo Huttoni Cassin*, still occurs in standard ornithologies. Hutton was an industrious collector of birds in Washington, D.C., as early as 1844; in California; and apparently again in Washington after his return. See Spencer F. Baird, *The Birds of North America* (Philadelphia, 1860), p. 339 and plate LXXVIII; also more than thirty references, throughout the text, to specimens obtained from Hutton. This volume is undoubtedly the source of the few lines accorded to him in Theodore S. Palmer, "Notes on Persons Whose Names Appear in the Nomenclature of California Birds," *The Condor*, XXX, 261-307.

[212]Rancho Santa Manuela, about 17,000 acres, granted to Francis Ziba Branch in 1837. Branch became one of the largest landholders of San Luis Obispo County. For a biographical sketch and portrait, see *History of San Luis Obispo County*, pp. 216-19.

couldn't get a shot. Some days afterwards Mr. Branch and I were going through the bushes at the head of the Arroyo Grande and came suddenly within twenty yards of a big black fellow, but he didn't stop long, as he was on the edge of the "monte."

But the greatest affair for me was the next day. We got to the house after dark and he didn't notice that the vaqueros had left the horses in the large corral, about 80 yards from the house, instead of putting them, as was customary, in the small one, the door of which joins a sleeping room. The next morning they were gone and the tracks of five or six Indians in the corral. We were soon fixing rifles, sending round for loose horses, &c., and, about 9 o'clock, several persons having come from neighboring ranchos, nine of us started. I went on a fine white horse that could not only travel far but run fast when required, and carried a light rifle (which I had used for some time) and my five-shooter. We soon found their "*medicine*"—a plume of crow feathers left in the road to give us bad luck in following them. We found a broad trail into Guasna,[213] where the road to the Tulares divides—one passing by San Miguel and coming into the plain just below the upper lake,[214] the other south easterly by the Panocha,[215] Lataillarde's farm,[216] and striking between

[213]Rancho Huasna, granted in 1843 to Isaac J. Sparks.

[214]Tulare Lake, called on the map in Lt. Derby's report, Taché Lake. Presumably the "two lower lakes" were Buena Vista and Kern.

[215]As indicating the probable route taken by the Branch party, the following passage (quoted from Derby's report [*Report of the Secretary of War* (32d Cong., 1st Sess.; Senate Ex. Doc. No. 110), p. 5]) is of interest: "We found but three passes through the coast range to the west of the road between the latitude of San Miguel and that of San Luis. These are the two roads, the one from San Miguel, the other from San Luis (via Paso de Roblas,) which meeting at a point called Estrella, form the pass of San Miguel; and a road passing through a cañada in the hills about fifteen miles east of San Luis, called the Penoche Pass, which debouches near the head of Buena Vista lake, and might with a little labor be made an excellent wagon path."

[216]Rancho Cuyama, formerly owned by Cesáreo Lataillade, who had died in 1849. (Bancroft, IV, 708.)

the two lower lakes. We followed the trail to the Cañada de los Alamos, a branch of the Santa Maria, where they had scattered the horses, that they might make no track, but, as it was evident they had gone out by the Panocha, and the Cañada was the shortest road, we kept on. We lost our way, once, and had to go back, but about sunset, after travelling 40 miles over the worst kind of a road, we looked down upon the "Cullama,"[217] as the upper plain of Santa Maria is called. We went down 6 or 7 miles and camped. The next morning we went to the spring and ruined corral, and there breakfasted, having become convinced that the caballada had not passed. We then started back to look for the other road, which comes over the mountains, and, while in a cañada one side of the road, about half the party was separated from us. We waited some time and called, but no one answered, and we were going out of the cañada when we saw one of the lost ones, a Sonorian, come down the mountain on a run. As he came up he said, "There goes the caballada"; and we five were in an instant on a small run for the mouth of the cañada. I couldn't see for the dust, but soon one who was a little ahead of me fired and, as we came to a turn in the road, I could see. The Indians, on foot and on horseback, had evidently not heard us nor seen our trail, for not a bow was strung, and when they found they were pursued they did not know we were so close behind; they plainly expected to carry off the horses, until this shot was fired, which, though it did no harm, whistled mighty close and let them know we were dangerously near. They then left the caballada, those on foot hiding in the bushes and those on horseback starting to run. Then we started, too, and for about three quarters of a mile I rode faster than I ever did before. We drove two from their horses to the "monte," and the other three kept on. Fearful

[217]The Cuyama Valley, at present lying mainly in Santa Barbara County, along the southern boundary of San Luis Obispo County.

that those who had hidden in the bushes might still carry off the horses, Mr. Branch & I, who were far ahead of the rest, returned and found everything right. Seven horses were missing out of about fifty—the three they carried of[f] and the others "quien sabe donde." They had eaten three little colts which were in the crowd. It is supposed that they stole the horses, not, as formerly, to eat, but to sell to passengers, as, tho' they had mounted the best horses the first day, they were then all mounted on mares and colts.

We returned to our camp of the previous night and kept a strict watch, all night, over the animals. The next day some seven who were mad with the Indians wanted to go on to the rancheria and punish them, but I thought, tho' I had done right in coming to take back the caballada, I had nothing to do with killing wild Indians in the Tulares and so I returned with the horses to the rancho. I was sorry afterwards that I did not go, tho' I still think I did right in not going, for they followed the trail to the middle lake[218] and there lost it, and returned, after passing through a very interesting country. They continued up the Cullama to the pass in the main ridge, which is just above probably the highest mountain in the coast range, San Armidio,[219] about twice as high as the rest of the ridge near, and covered with snow in the end of April. It is also know[n] as the "Silver mine," but I don't know that it was ever worked. They brought specimens of rocks—a very pretty striped, and another spotted, granite; and a third looked like soapstone but much harder and not greasy to the touch, containing a good deal of mica. I saw one or two flowers which I did not know, but either could not get them or they broke up in my pocket. I have a cypress (Thuya) from San Armidio, different, I

[218]Perhaps Goose Lake, between lakes Tulare and Buena Vista.

[219]Hutton is evidently referring here to San Emigdio Peak, 7,415 feet elevation, in southern Kern County, near the Ventura County line.

think, from the Monterey one; and, for the first time, this spring I saw Brown's peony[220] very abundant and have specimens both in flower and fruit, and some few other little [word illegible].

I havn't yet seen the law about land titles but I must keep my eyes open to see if there is a chance for me. Unless people change their minds, in consequence of this, I will have work for two or three months yet.

I must get specimens of this panocha cane,[221] which looks like a large grass, about 6 to 8 feet high. I havn't even looked at it close, tho' I passed thro' such quantities, but I had enough to do to see that my horse didn't get stuck in the mud.

Mr. B—— is just starting for San Luis & I havn't time to commence another sheet, but I have lots more to say and will have another written soon. . . .

Arroyo Grande, May 24th, 1851.

My dear Mother,

I wrote to Uncle a few days ago, but not only [do] we have a regular mail to Monterey, now, but a friend who is going up in a day or two will take this. I leave, this afternoon, to go to a place called the *Huehuero*,[222] about 35 miles from here, which I am to survey, but I will come back here to do all the work except notes and sketches. With your letter, I received one from Mrs. Canby (who, I suppose, you will see before you receive this), which was the first information I had of their being about to leave. I was on my own account right sorry; on hers, right glad. Not only has she been very kind but has given me a great deal of very good advice, and the Major is the same. I shall miss them both when I go north again.

[220] Jepson, *Manual*, p. 373.

[221] Variant spelling, *panoja*. The Spanish word means a plant having a seed spike, or head, resembling that of maize, millet, or panic grass. Not identified.

[222] Rancho Huer-Huero, in San Luis Obispo County, 15,684 acres, once belonging to Mission San Miguel, was granted in 1842-44 to José Mariano Bonilla. It had been purchased by Francis Z. Branch.

You allude to the stories about my being in love. Almost everybody in Monterey believed it, and some that I was married, but neither has happened yet. The origin of the tale was this: When Mrs. Burton was asking me about the people of San Luis I spoke very highly of this young lady, and Mrs. B. asked me if I was going to marry her. I replied that she was a little child, only twelve years old, and received for answer, "In four years she will be old enough, & you, too, you are too young to marry now." Afterwards, in a letter, I told her I would follow her advice and not be married for four years, and, as the Captn. and she *plagued* me about it a good deal, others thought they certainly knew my secrets and it must be so. I thought you had received my letter in which I abused them so, as I recollect doing in one, at least. But my sweetheart wasn't so bad as the rest. As to education, I thought they had a very decent one for Californians. They can make very pretty letters, but neither spell, nor even understand what they read. The oldest is only 14, but, as they belong to the *aristocracy*, people think that everybody wants to marry them, and the usual attentions paid by a gentleman to his partner in a cotillion are enough to convince everybody that he is over head & ears in love.[223] . . . And, although it is possible I may marry in California, I don't think it will be with anybody born in the country.

As to San José lots, I did get into a scrape with them, about taxes, but they are all right now. A mighty nice farm of a league square was sold here, two or three days ago, at auction, for $1400. I knew nothing of it or I would have been there, as I have had my eye on it ever since I knew that it must be sold, but I didn't expect the sale so soon. I couldn't have got it, for there was a good deal of trickery about it. Persons were present ready to give four or five thousand dollars for it. I expect Jim's

[223]Evidently he is referring to daughters of Capt. John Wilson, whose ranches he had surveyed. See the letter of Dec. 23, 1850.

overland trip was only imaginary & that it won't come to pass. When I last heard from him (indirectly) he was well and doing well. One reason why I would like to get a little piece of land is that I could have him with me, and we could, I think, do well.

. . . .

To William Rich

San José (New Almaden), December 11', 1851.

Dear Uncle,

I have nothing to write about that will interest you, but I can't let a mail go without saying something.

I received Mother's letter of Oct. 9th a day or two ago—in which she speaks of the disadvantages of buying land in California. I believe I have since explained why I did so; it was that, by buying half of four leagues of land for sixty dollars, I collected three hundred of a debt of six hundred due me from San Luis County. I hope I will make something by it, but, if I should lose it altogether, it would have been the best thing to be done under the circumstances.

I have [had] no time to devote to natural history for some time past; since I came to this place I have only been to the mine and to San José. I have made a few sketches and would send them, but I want to finish them, more, first. I also left some in Monterey, by mistake, which I could finish if I had them here. At present Mr. Young,[224] the administrator, is in San Francisco sick; Halleck in Sonoma, judge advocate of a court for the trial of Derby & Hooker;[225] and I have the office-work, which is very much behindhand, to bring up, and am con-

[224]John Young (1824?-64), nephew of Capt. John Wilson, of San Luis Obispo County, and, like his uncle, a trader and master of vessels. In his later years he was superintendent of the New Almaden Mine. (Bancroft, V, 783.)

[225]Lt. George H. Derby was tried by court-martial at Sonoma, in Nov., 1851, on charges preferred by Lt.-Col. Joseph Hooker, but escaped with a reprimand. (George R. Stewart, *John Phoenix, Esq.* [New York, 1937], pp. 79-92.)

sequently quite busy. Capt. Burton is in the court in Benecia. The papers spoke of his company as about to go to San Diego to fight the Indians who have become hostile, but, as they are now quieting down, I suppose he will not go.[226] Murray was at the Gila, in rather a tight place, at last accounts.[227]

Letters, 1852

Nuevo Almaden, February 29th, 1852.

My dear Mother,

. . . .

I heard from Jim in S. Luis, a few days ago, and on the same day saw "J. B. Hutton" 's name as a passenger to S. Francisco by the coast steamer. I suppose it to be his name, but he has not written from that place. He had engaged to do some surveying and wanted a compass. He is rather tired of San Luis, but don't know what to do if he leaves it.

If there were not so much risk I would apply to Mr. King[228] for a contract for surveying, but I don't know whether I could make anything out of it, and might lose. My only object in doing so would be to have Jim with me.

. . . .

I was a little surprised to find that Grace Church,[229] in San Francisco, was not sold, as I wrote you, some time ago, was

[226]An Indian uprising occurred in southern California in Nov., 1851—centering at Warner's Ranch, in San Diego County. It was checked by prompt military action, and several Indians and one white man were tried and executed for their part in it. (Joseph J. Hill, *The History of Warner's Ranch* [Los Angeles, 1927], pp. 137-42.)

[227]The Yuma and Cocopa Indians were giving trouble near Camp Yuma at this time. (*Ibid.*, p. 138.)

[228]Samuel D. King, U.S. surveyor-general for California.

[229]Grace Church, the second Episcopal church in San Francisco, was organized by Rev. John L. Ver Mehr, a missionary, who arrived in San Francisco

the case. The members took shares in it to save it. It is still deeply in debt. It is a beautiful building, though slight, being of wood covered with iron, and, as the ground is much lower than the grade of the street, it is raised on piles driven into the ground. Dr. Mines' (Trinity) new church[230] is said to be beautiful—the handsomest in the country; it is nearer the water. Grace Church is pretty high up. If I go to San Francisco, again, I must get some prints or daguerrotypes for Uncle, to show him the changes in old, familiar places. Grace and Old Trinity churches are on the corners of the streets running west from the south side of the "Plaza," and about as far back as the low ground at the foot of the sand hill on the road to Presidio.

I have not heard from any of our friends for some time. Mr. Bestor was in San Francisco about two weeks ago & heard that Mrs. Willie was quite sick.

. . . .

We have just recd. Como. Stockton's speech on the petition to allow flogging in the navy. Every[one] laughs at "gasey Bob" 's mention of Hull in the Constitution, and himself in the miserable little skirmish of San Gabriel,[231] at the same time, and how pitifully he complains of the way Mr. Badger uses him up.

---

in Sept., 1849. The first building, known as Grace Chapel, was opened for services on Dec. 29, 1849. A larger building was erected in 1851, on Powell Street. (Douglas O. Kelley, *History of the Diocese of California* [San Francisco, 1915], pp. 4, 341-42.)

[230]Trinity Church was organized in July, 1849—the first Episcopal church in the city. Its rector was Rev. Flavel Scott Mines, who had preceded Dr. Ver Mehr by two months, coming by way of Panama. The first church building was erected in 1849, at the corner of Powell and Jackson Streets, and a larger building on Pine Street in 1851. (*Ibid.*, pp. 4, 342-43.)

[231]In his speech in the Senate, on Jan. 7, 1852, Senator (formerly Commodore) Robert Field Stockton, of New Jersey, referred twice to the passage of the San Gabriel River by the sailors under his command, on Jan. 8, 1847, preceding the recapture of Los Angeles. His speech was replied to by Senator George E. Badger, of North Carolina.

San Francisco, May 31', 1852.

My dear Mother,

I received your letters & Ellen's of April 22d & 24', in less than one month; they, having been too late for the regular mail, came in the Illinois[232] and Golden Gate, in 25½ days from New York. . . .

. . . .

Since I last wrote I have spent ten or twelve days at New Almaden—riding on horseback and drinking mineral water all the time—and came back very much better in health than when I left to go there.

Yesterday (Whitsunday) the "Alleghanians"[233] sang at Grace Church, and I heartily wished them somewhere else; I would much rather have had the choir of the church. They sing so well they would have no instrumental music—which is absolutely necessary, I think, in some chants, psalms, & hymns, as in the *Venite exultemus*, . . . I was very much pleased with the sermon by Dr. Vermehr[234] . . . very excellent and much of it

[232]A steamer of the U.S. Mail Steamship Company, sailing from New York to Chagres, on the Atlantic side of the Isthmus of Panama. The "Golden Gate," of the Pacific Mail Steamship Company, sailing between Panama and San Francisco, had arrived at the latter port on May 22, 1852. (Wiltsee, *Gold Rush Steamers*, pp. 30, 80.)

[233]A group of singers who began giving concerts in New York City in 1846 and continued until 1869. In the spring of 1852 they visited California. They were known later as the Swiss bell ringers and vocalists. (MacMinn, *Theater of the Golden Era*, pp. 393-94.)

[234]Rev. John L. (born Jean Leonhard Henri Corneille) Ver Mehr (1808?-86), a native of Belgium, who had emigrated to the United States in 1843. He taught and preached in Burlington, New Jersey, until 1849, when he was sent as a missionary to establish an Episcopal church in San Francisco. He was rector of Grace Church until succeeded by Bishop William Ingraham Kip in 1854. During several years thereafter he conducted a girls' school, St. Mary's Hall, in Sonoma and San Francisco. (J. L. Ver Mehr, *Checkered Life: In the Old and New World* [San Francisco, 1877]; William I. Kip, *The Early Days of My Episcopate* [New York, 1892], pp. 94-96.)

very beautiful, tho' few persons would think so, on account of the Doctor's bad pronunciation of English.

There is a good deal of excitement, here, about Mr. Gwin's squatter law, introduced in the Senate in April last.[235] He probably expects to become popular among the squatters, but he has missed it this time, as he has excluded from the privileges of his law all those who committed their depredations since the 3rd of March, 1851, and he is being very severely handled by editors & others who can get a chance. Mr. Peachy[236] has written an excellent article, but, as published in today's Herald, it is very much mutilated and some of the best parts of it left out. Dr. Ryder,[237] of Georgetown, preached yesterday in the city. His sermon was a very excellent one as reported in the Herald. I will send a copy if I can get one.

I saw Mrs. Willey a few days ago, and learned from her that Snowdon Bacon[238] & his wife were neighbors. I have not called there, yet, but will do so soon. . . .

Jim seemed to be very well when he wrote; he has not done anything definite with regard to my affairs in San Luis but says he will arrange them all, soon.

. . . .

[235]This was a bill introduced in the U.S. Senate to give valid title, to eighty acres each, to squatters on Mexican grants; holders of the grants were to be permitted to select an equal area of other public lands. The bill failed of passage.

[236]Archibald C. Peachy (1820-83), then, or later, a member of the law firm of Halleck, Peachy, Billings & Park.

[237]Dr. James Ryder (1800-1860), president of Georgetown College, 1841-43, 1848-51, and superior of the Jesuit order in the United States, 1843-45. He was in San Francisco four months during 1852, on business connected with the society.

[238]J. Snowden Bacon, who arrived in San Francisco in Aug., 1849, appears to have been in business there in 1852. (Society of California Pioneers, *Constitution and By-laws . . . and List of Members* [San Francisco, 1912], p. 93; James M. Parker, *The San Francisco Directory for . . . 1852-53*, pp. 34, 107.)

San Francisco, June 25th, 1852.

My dear Mother,

. . . .

The "Northerner"[239] arrived on Wednesday of last week. On Friday I went out to Happy Valley to call on Mrs. Willey's newly arrived sister. She was not at home, but from Mr. Willey I learned that another little lady had appeared in the family—Mrs. W. had had a little girl the day previous.

. . . Last evening I called again at Mr. Willey's and had the pleasure of meeting Miss Jeffers. I was very much pleased, indeed, and agreeably disappointed—from what I had heard of her from officers and others who were acquainted with her, I did not expect to see such a pretty, intelligent, and agreeable lady as she seems to be.

You may be surprised to see my letter dated so much before the mail-day, but I am going to the mine again, tomorrow, to look after things while Mr. Young, the administrator, is in San Francisco. You ask if I do better here than at the mine—I get the same pay, being furnished with a room and my mess bill paid, in addition to the $100 per month. The work here is more confining, tho' Capt. Halleck is very kind and considerate and, when he thinks I have been working too hard, he won't give me anything to do; but the other advantages more than counterbalance the difference of climate, &c.

I have visited, several times, at Dr. Ver Mehr's and have been very much pleased with the Dr. and Mrs. Ver Mehr. They are both Germans, and speak English with a *decided* German pronunciation.

. . . .

[239]Put in service between Panama and San Francisco by the Empire City Line in the summer of 1850, it was sold in the fall of the same year to the Pacific Mail Steamship Company.

This, I hope, will go by the Golden Gate on the 28th inst.... The Golden Gate and Winfield Scott (opposition line)[240] are on a trial of speed, this trip; the latter leaves on the 26th, but Captain Patterson[241] of the *G. G.* expects to be at Panama a day ahead of the Scott.

. . . .

Los Angeles, Oct. 8', 1852.

My dear Mother,

I have not heard from you since I last wrote, and it will be too late if I wait for my letters until the 11th. I heard from Jim a few days ago, but only that he was well, & still in San Luis, trying to dispose of his and my county scrip. I have nothing new to tell you, except it be my excursion to the Mormon settlement at San Bernardino, with Capt. Halleck and others. We were absent from this place about five days, but four of them were passed on the road. The first day we started late, passed the Mission of San Gabriel (formerly the richest of all) and, passing many camps of immigrants, stopped for the night at the rancho of Mr. Roland,[242] La Puente. Here we were very kindly received & well taken care of, & we found better grapes than any in Los Angeles. The next day, about twelve miles was among the hills, and we passed several fine gardens & ranchos; the remainder of the distance, 30 miles, was over a sandy plain,

[240]The "Winfield Scott," a new vessel of the New York and San Francisco Steamship Company, had nearly the same tonnage as the "Golden Gate" and was making the run between San Francisco and Panama in about the same time (14 days).

[241]Carlile Pollock Patterson (1816-81), lieutenant in the U.S. navy until his resignation in Sept., 1853. Before this he entered the service of the Pacific Mail Steamship Company, in which he continued until 1861.

[242]John Rowland (1791?-1873), a native of Maryland, with William Workman, led a party from Taos, N. Mex., to southern California, in 1842. In 1845 Rowland and Workman were granted La Puente Rancho, lying about twenty miles east of Los Angeles and comprising nearly 49,000 acres. (Guinn, *Historical and Biographical Record of Los Angeles*, pp. 663-64.)

without water—leaving the recently deserted military post of the "Chino"[243] about 8 or 9 miles to the right, the mountain range being as far off on the other side. We arrived at the camp very late & had no time to see much, that night. We stayed all the next day. The number of inhabitants is about six hundred, who live mostly in their fort—a square formed by driving in posts very close together; their houses are mere shanties, and they are not very comfortably situated; they have raised a very large crop of wheat & were very busy getting it threshed & cleaned. One of their head men—he is one of the Twelve Apostles—is a General Rich[244]—no relation of ours, I hope. I notice that the Apostles are always the richest men of the party; there are two here—they own the mill, the wheat machines, have the best houses & the largest crops of anybody.

The people are mostly simple and ignorant, but very hard workers—and that keeps them out of mischief. They get along very happily. After stopping there a day we returned by the same road.

I have met, here, a Mr. Rose,[245] a lawyer who is a great churchman and somewhat acquainted in Washington. He &

243"In September, 1850, a post of the United States Regular Army was established at Chino, a captain, two lieutenants, an army surgeon [James T. Overstreet], and twenty privates being stationed there. This post was maintained for two years, when it was removed to the Robidoux Rancho on the Jurupa grant." (Beattie, *Heritage of the Valley*, p. 134.)

244The present city of San Bernardino was founded by a colony of Mormons, who came from Salt Lake City in the spring of 1851, led by two of the Twelve Apostles of the Mormon church, Charles C. Rich and Amasa M. Lyman. The settlement took its name from the Rancho San Bernardino, 35,500 acres, which was purchased by Rich and Lyman from the Lugo family for $77,500. (*Ibid.*, pp. 170-91; John Henry Evans, *Charles Coulson Rich* [New York, 1936], pp. 199-225.)

245Julius K. Rose, at the time a member of the firm of McAllister, Edwards & Rose, of San Francisco. He was one of a group of lawyers who came from there to Los Angeles to attend the sessions of the U.S. Commission on Private Land Claims. (San Francisco directories, 1852-61/62; *Los Angeles Star*, Aug. 28, 1852.)

Mr. French[246] were college mates together. We were talking about people at home, this morning. He says Mrs. French promised to pick out a wife for him and he is going on to Washington next spring—to see about it.

He tells me—what I had not heard before—that since Dr. Mines'[247] death Dr. Southard has been called to Trinity Church, & Bishop Hawks to Grace Chapel.

I hav'n't heard of Mrs. Willey, nor her sister, since I left San Francisco. Capt. & Mrs. Burton were on a pleasure excursion to a rancho just over the boundary line—in Lower California. Halleck is here and well. The place is very dull, and unfortunately I have very few books with me. I had no room to stow them.

. . . .

Santa Barbara, Nov. 26, 1852.

My dear Mother,

I believe you did not get anything from me by the last mail. We were about three weeks without a steamer—the Seabird,[248] on her way down, broke her shaft, had to throw overboard part of her cargo, and was very near going ashore. She is expected in here to day. I hope she will come—I am tired of this place. The Ohio[249] came down, several days ago, & goes up today. I would go in her but I expect letters by the Seabird.

[246]Rev. John William French (1810-71), rector of Epiphany Church, Washington, D.C., 1842-56. He graduated from Trinity College, Hartford, Conn., in 1832. No person named Rose appears in the list of Trinity College students of this period.

[247]Rev. Flavel Scott Mines, first rector of Trinity Church, San Francisco, was a graduate of Princeton Theological Seminary, and pastor of a Presbyterian church in New York City for several years before taking orders in the Protestant Episcopal church. He died in San Francisco, Aug. 8, 1852, and was succeeded, in Feb., 1853, by Rev. Christopher B. Wyatt.

[248]A steamer plying between San Francisco and San Diego.

[249]This vessel, belonging to the Pacific Mail Steamship Company, arrived in

We have had some rain & storms, lately, but the weather is beautiful now. I hav'n't heard any news for a long time & nothing happens here. The only "news" is the burning of Sacramento city & a block in San Francisco, right next to Halleck's office. The Land Commission does not meet here—and they will go up in the Ohio, I suppose.

. . . .

. . . I see Catherine Hayes[250] has arrived in San Francisco. I hope I may hear her sing. . . .

San Francisco, Dec. 15th, 1852.

My dear Mother,

I received yours of Nov. 4' by the last mail, and yesterday one from Uncle, of Nov. 12. He was very well, then, but very busy. . . . We arrived here from Santa Barbara on Sunday week; and I don't know how long I shall stay. We are having rather bad weather this month—it rains almost every day.

I was invited, day before yesterday, to a *teaparty* at Mrs. Willey's. I went, & passed a very pleasant evening. There were a good many ladies, and the best in San Francisco. . . . I received a letter from Capt. Burton, about 10 days ago, saying that Mrs. Burton had a fine little boy, and was doing very well. She dislikes San Diego, very much, but tries to be reconciled to it.

Doña Angustias, who I saw in Santa Barbara, was very much

San Francisco from New York in Jan., 1851, and ran between San Francisco and southern California and Mexican ports.

[250]Catherine Hayes (1820-61), prima donna, was born in Ireland and studied in France and Italy. Her first appearance in the United States was in New York City, in Sept., 1851. She came to California in Nov., 1852, under contract with P. T. Barnum, to give a series of sixty concerts, and sang in San Francisco, Sacramento, and Grass Valley. Her concerts were enormously popular and some seats sold at auction for as high as $1,200. She visited California again in 1854. (MacMinn, *op. cit.*, pp. 388-92.)

disgusted. Don Manuel had sold both his ranchos for $45,000, about one third of their value.[251]

He is frightened to death, almost—fearful that his daughters will marry Protestants; and he will not attempt to speculate with his money, lest the Protestants should cheat him out of it. The person who cheated him out of his ranchos was recommended by Father Ryder, of Georgetown. He has two smart, interesting daughters, who are very much afraid that he will try to take them to Mexico, or, at least, away from Santa Barbara; but I do not believe their grandfather[252] will allow it. He (the old gentleman) has been very sick—not expected to live—but seems as well as ever again. He is the greatest man for prayers that ever lived—in the morning, before and after dinner, after coffee at 3 o'clock, & before and after supper, beside what answers to the blessing and thanksgiving at every meal.

I stopped in Monterey, on my way up, and saw almost all the folks, but it looks deserted.

I find that the ladies are getting up a fair for Christmas week, for the benefit of Grace Church. I have been told that, since Mr. Mines' death, Mr. Southard, of New York, has been requested to come to San Francisco, & also Bp. Hawkes—the first declined, the second said he would come (of course temporarily), if he could find any person to take his place during his absence from his diocese. I believe it is now resolved that Bp. Johns, of Virginia, shall be asked.

Halleck talks of going home in March, by way of Acapulco, and, if I do not go before, I have no doubt I shall go then. . . . If I find there is a good chance for anything here, such as

[251]Hutton's old Monterey friends, Doña Angustias and Don Manuel Jimeno Casarin. The two ranchos were Santa Paula y Saticoy, nearly 18,000 acres, in Ventura County, and the Jimeno Rancho, about 49,000 acres, in Colusa and Yolo counties. Don Manuel went to Mexico, early in 1853, and died there the same year.

[252]José de la Guerra y Noriega. See above, n. 113.

surveying, I will only consider it a visit home; but I expect I will [remain] if I can find employment.

I hear a great deal said about Colonel & Mrs. Canby coming back to this country. You don't say anything about it and I suppose it is not so. I sent to Mrs. Canby a drawing which I owed her, before I went to Los Angeles. I wonder if she has received it.

. . . .

Letters, January-February, 1853

San Francisco, Jany 31', 1853.

My dear Mother,

Since my last, I have recd. yours of Dec. 18th, but none from Uncle. Jim is here at present; he arrived about a week ago, from Santa Cruz, where the vessel he was on went ashore. He is not doing anything particular at present. . . .

. . . .

We have had some fine sermons from Dr. Ver Mehr, lately. . . . Mr. Moore,[253] at Trinity, has preached two or three sermons during the last two weeks—which have induced some of the vestry to request him not to preach any more. He asked to be allowed until Mr. Wyatt's arrival—who is expected on the next steamer. His sermons were such as all good churchmen believe but do not say openly, and he drew necessary inferences from established doctrines, which very much offended some people. . . .

I have been fortunate with regard to the concerts by Miss Hayes—I have been four or five times, and every time but one

[253]Rev. J. Moore. See Parker, *San Francisco Directory . . . 1852-53*, p. 79, and App., p. 21. Moore is listed in that directory as pastor of Trinity Church, but no mention of him is found in Kelley, *History of the Diocese of California*. In the *San Francisco Herald*, Jan. 16, 1853, the name appears as Rev. J. D. Moore.

was presented with a ticket. I heard Lucrecia Borgia about 10 days ago. I was not so much pleased with it as with others, on account of the very excellence of the performance. It is very tragic and was very well acted as well as sung. . . . I heard her also, one evening, in Kathleen, in "The Last Rose of Summer," "Comin' thro' the Rye," & "Don Pasquale." She has been singing, last week, from a sweet opera, "Linda de Chamouni." I have not heard her. Biscaccianti[254] (who goes tomorrow) used to sing some pieces from it.

I find that the expense of travelling from Acapulco to Mexico is considerably more than I heard from Uncle. It is expensive by Panama, too, and I think that if Halleck does not go by Mexico, I will, by Nicaragua.[255] . . .

. . . .

San Francisco, Feby. 15', 1853.

My dear Mother,

I was in hopes that the Golden Gate would arrive soon enough for me to get my letters before writing, but it is now too late to expect it. Since I last wrote, nothing of much interest has occurred. . . . I have heard several persons speak of going through Mexico, about the middle of next month, and I expect I can form one of a good party—which will probably be both safer and less expensive, as there are many items which would be as great for a single traveller as for ten. . . .

[254]Eliza Biscacciante (1824-96) was born in Boston and made her debut in New York City in 1847. She arrived in California in Feb., 1852, and sang to crowded houses, in San Francisco and other places, for about a year. Sailing for Peru in Feb., 1853, she returned to California, in 1859, to find her popularity greatly diminished. (*San Francisco Theatre Research*, 1st Ser., Vol. VII, pp. 19-30.)

[255]Early in 1853 the competition of the Vanderbilt Line, routing its passengers through Nicaragua, with the Pacific Mail Steamship Company, using the Panama route, had reduced the through fare to New York to $100. (Wiltsee, *op. cit.*, pp. 90-92.)

We, or rather *they*, have had a very unpleasant occurrence in Trinity Church. In the first place, Mr. Moore, who was engaged to act until their rector should arrive, was on general principles opposed to fairs unless absolutely necessary, and, when the ladies had one without consulting him, several notices disapproving of it were published in the daily papers; again he preached a sermon, in which, as I was told, he said the various bodies of dissenters could not be considered as belonging to the church; the next day, he was requested by the vestry, in some very insolent resolutions, not to preach any more in the church; he asked what charge was brought against him; they at first would make none, afterwards said he was *supposed* to be the author of the newspaper articles upon the fair; he said they had no right to suppose so, and he did not write them. The next Sunday he preached again; a few days afterwards, he was told he *should not* officiate again; and, the next time, he found the door locked. The members of the vestry were very anxious to convince Dr. Ver Mehr that they were right, and, a report having been circulated that he had approved their course, he wrote a letter to the vestry, in which he said he could not, and did not, approve of their "ejecting a presbyter from the altar," without making any definite charge against him, and in so unauthorized a manner; this rather startled them; they had not looked upon it in that light before; but the Reverend Fathers Clark[256] and Morgan[257]–the first in civil life, the second a missionary *loafing* in San Francisco, when there is so much work to be done through the country–took part in the matter, the latter personally, the former both personally & by letter, saying, among other things, that "the minister was highly

[256]Rev. Orange Clark, chaplain of the U.S. Marine Hospital.

[257]Probably Rev. John Morgan, who preached in Stockton in 1851-53. (Kelley, *op. cit.*, p. 402; George H. Tinkham, *History of Stockton* [San Francisco, 1880], p. 338.)

culpable who would not yield to the wishes of a respectable *minority*"; and they offered to put Mr. Moore out of church by force if he should attempt to enter. Some 14 or 15 wished to call a parish meeting but the vestry would not, and Messrs. Clark & Morgan became suddenly very high churchmen—said that a parish meeting was without warrant or precedent, was Congregationalism, &c. Dr. Ver Mehr's opinion was asked, and, in a letter to one of the applicants, he cited precedents, even in Grace Church & by its constitution; said that, if a minister was culpable, so was a vestry that would not yield to the wishes of a respectable minority, &c.; and so the matter stands until the new rector arrives—who is expected this week. I am pleased with *our* rector's course, and everybody else thinks he has acted very well, under the circumstances. . . . I think the Doctor is an admirable preacher, though not very popular on account of the difficulty of understanding his broken English—but it only requires a little practice. We have service on Wednesdays and Fridays of every week, but no lectures, as the church is so out-of-the-way that few could or would attend at night.

. . . .

I was at Mrs. Willey's, last evening. . . . They expect, daily, Major Eaton's[258] family—to remain with them probably until their house is vacated in April.

. . . .

. . . I met Lt. Bonnycastle[259] a few days ago; he said he had seen you in Washington, tho' a long time ago. Capt. Smith[260] I did not see; he was only here a day or two.

[258]Maj. Amos Beebe Eaton (1806-77) was chief of commissariat of the Department of the Pacific, 1851-55.

[259]John C. Bonnycastle, first lieutenant and adjutant of Stevenson's regiment of New York volunteers; later lieutenant of the 4th U.S. infantry.

[260]Perhaps Capt. Andrew Jackson Smith, 1st U.S. dragoons, later a major general of volunteers during the Civil War.

Other Writings by William R. Hutton on California

So far as has been learned, Mr. Hutton never published anything regarding his experiences in California. He left, however, in addition to his letters and diaries, several manuscript sketches, based on those experiences, but apparently written at a later date. These papers, photostatic copies of which are in the Huntington Library, are described below:

[Trial and attempted execution of a horse thief at Monterey, February, 1849, involving the court-martial of Lieutenant Matthew R. Stevenson.] 2 pp. For letters relating to the incident and the ensuing court-martial, see Zachary Taylor, *California and New Mexico. Message from the President* (Washington, 1850), pp. 693-94, 896, 915. An English artist, William Redmond Ryan, living in Monterey at the time, gives his impressions of the affair, in *Personal Adventures in Upper and Lower California, in 1848-9* (London, 1850), II, 118-24.

[Description and characterization of the Spanish Californians, especially the women, with mention of several individuals.] 4 pp.

The Wedding. [Account of the festivities at the wedding of María Josefa Dana and Henry Amos Tefft, at Nipomo Rancho, July, 1850.] 3 pp.

[Narrative of a horseback ride, with William L. Beebee, from San Luis Obispo to Monterey, in September, 1850. (This is also described in Hutton's letter of September 30, 1850.) Supposed ride of Victor Linares from Los Angeles to Monterey, and return, in six days, in 1849. Incidents at Francis Z. Branch's Rancho Santa Manuela, in 1851, including another account of the pursuit of Indian raiders, described in Hutton's letter of May 18, 1851.] 8 pp.

[Story of an alleged attempt, in 1852, to sell to the city of San Francisco a document purporting to be a grant to the city of two square leagues of pueblo lands.] 2 pp.

[Anecdotes concerning Rev. Walter Colton, alcalde of Monterey, 1846-48.] 3 pp.

APPENDIX

Appendix

Report of Paymaster William Rich to the Paymaster General, 1848

THE following report of William Rich was discovered during the editing of the Hutton diaries and letters and is reprinted here, not only as supplementary to them, but for its statements concerning difficulties facing the military authorities after the discovery of gold. The letter was apparently first printed in the *National Intelligencer*, of Washington, D.C., in its triweekly edition of January 23, 1849, and was reprinted in two contemporary works, Joseph Warren Revere's *A Tour of Duty in California* (New York and Boston, 1849), pp. 255-56, and Jessy Quinn Thornton's *Oregon and California in 1848* (New York, 1849), II, 339-40. Whether it was reproduced in other newspapers or books has not been ascertained.

Monterey, (Cal.) Oct. 23, 1848.

General:

I arrived here on the 18th instant, from San Diego, and have paid the four companies of the 1st New York regiment[261] in full, and they have all started for the gold mines. The three companies composing the command of Lieut. Col. Burton are now here,[262] and will be mustered out to-day or to-morrow, and paid by Major Hill immediately, as the residents are extremely anxious to get rid of them: they have the place in their power. Nearly all the men of company "F," 3d artillery, have deserted. We have the Ohio, Warren, Dale, Lexington, and Southampton in port; but they *cannot land a man,* as they desert as soon as they set foot on shore. The only thing the ships could do, in case of an outbreak, would be to fire upon the town. The volunteers at Santa Barbara, Los Angeles, &c., behaved very well—no murmuring or difficulties of any kind

[261]Company F, stationed at Santa Barbara; Companies E and G, at Los Angeles; and Company I, at San Diego. (Bancroft, V, 515.)

[262]Companies A, B, and D, which had been in Lower California. (*Ibid.*)

with them; they complained that they were not allowed travelling allowance.

The funds from Mazatlan have at last reached here; the amount is $130,000. It arrived very opportunely, as we have expended nearly all we had. The amount is a great deal more than will be required, as there are at present but two companies in California—one of 1st dragoons, the other of 3d artillery; the latter reduced to a mere skeleton by desertion, and the former in a fair way to share the same fate. I should suppose $20,000 would be sufficient to pay the present force (provided the companies are filled up) for a year. Treasury notes are good for nothing now; bills on the United States could not be negotiated on any terms. Gold dust can be purchased for eight or ten dollars the ounce, and it is said to be worth $18 in the United States; consequently, all remittances are made in it.

Col. Mason, and most of the army officers, are at Fort Sutter. Commodore Jones thinks it would be very imprudent to bring the public funds on shore, except in such sums as may be required for immediate use. He does not like to leave a ship here, on account of the difficulty of keeping the men.

The gold fever rages as bad as ever, and the quantity collected has not diminished, but increased. Provisions, clothing, and all the necessaries of life are at most exorbitant prices. Living was always expensive in this country, but now it passes all reason—board four dollars per day, washing five to six dollars per dozen. Merchants' clerks are receiving from $1,800 to $3,000 per annum salary. What the government will do for civil officers, I do not know. Salaries will have to correspond with the times. The pay of governors, judges, &c., as allowed in the United States, will hardly compare with that paid to salesmen and shop clerks here. I am, sir, respectfully, your obedient servant,

William Rich, A. P., U.S.A.

Gen. N. Towson, Paymaster Gen., U.S.A.,
Washington.